GLOBAL WARMING

GLOBAL WARMING

A REAL THREAT

Duncan Ewing

GLOBAL WARMING
A REAL THREAT

iUniverse books may be ordered through booksellers or by contacting:

iUniverse
1663 Liberty Drive
Bloomington, IN 47403
www.iuniverse.com
1-800-Authors (1-800-288-4677)

Because of the dynamic nature of the Internet, any web addresses or links contained in
this book may have changed since publication and may no longer be valid. The views
expressed in this work are solely those of the author and do not necessarily reflect the views
of the publisher, and the publisher hereby disclaims any responsibility for them.

Any people depicted in stock imagery provided by Getty Images are models,
and such images are being used for illustrative purposes only.
Certain stock imagery © Getty Images.

ISBN: 978-1-5320-8599-4 (sc)
ISBN: 978-1-5320-8600-7 (e)

Print information available on the last page.

iUniverse rev. date: 10/16/2019

The topic of global warming is interesting in that it determines what is happening to our climate today. We don't know why it is so strange in weather due to our inability to comprehend what is happening. However, as the globe heats up and the disaster effects start to surface, it seems evident that the threat is very real. People need to realize the damage that is causing our planet to spin out of control. As we realize that this world is in dire need of change, we see our precious globe that god created go into ruins. With it seems an interesting task to solve a problem that is only getting worse. The question then is how far gone is this world in terms of fossil fuels and greenhouse gases.

As BC saw a roller coaster of weather in 2019 starting with a 1st half of winter that was very mild and spring-like. However, on February 3rd the shift occurred, and the Jetstream went to favor a cold and snowy pattern that wouldn't break until March 10th. In February alone BC broke all time snow and cold records in general in what is usually a mild and wet pattern from the pacific. As these records were shattered, the concern was is this the new norm that winters in BC will be cold and snowy and spring-fall warm and dry. The reality is that possibly this is only one bad year, and everything will return to normal in 2020 or is a recurring situation due to climate change. However, it is important to note that in March when the shift back into warmer weather occurred, we broke many record high temperatures for the month of March alone.

So, as we have seen with the wicked weather BC has experienced in 2019, it is evident that our planet is unstable, and the Jetstream is reacting to the changes in the atmospheric temperatures. In terms of what we know from El Niño winters in

BC, never has a warm pattern favored cold and snowy. Usually El Nino is warm and dry in BC and western Canada due to the Jetstream keeping the moisture and cold away from BC blocking it back north. However, in 2019 this didn't happen properly and as a result the weather favored the iconic Jetstream that only was stagnant meaning it didn't move until spring eventually started. In fact, it was the coldest and snowiest El Nino winter BC has experienced since 1950. The reality is that even La Nina the last 2 years back to back didn't produce such a consistent cold and snowy pattern. Usually when we get arctic outbreaks in the winter, they last 1-2 weeks then go back to being mild and wet.

It is evident wicked weather has hammered not just BC but the whole globe and it is getting much worse due to the emissions of greenhouse gases and CO_2 into the atmosphere. Thus, such a trend is concerning because it seems that our globe is angry with us for hurting it that way we are. Humans are so selfish in that they cannot see the damage caused by their choices daily. Scientists have said for years ditch the vehicle and walk or take public transit, yet people don't get the message. This book is like many others on the market that our world is suffering because folks won't open their eyes and look around at the extreme weather happening. It is time to act now before it is too late to go back, and this is the future folks and the science backs it up.

It is evident that the topics our climate change that will be covered in this book are not just another shake up but the reality that has been occurring for the last 200 years. If we are having this extreme weather in 2019, then how bad will it be in 50 years? That is the question that people are asking based on how quickly it has occurred that climate change is worsening and nothing seems to be working to solve this trend. We as the citizens of the earth must realize that as the planet warms, many nasty things will increase and result in our planet being too hot to sustain any sort of human life. However, as this issue isn't being addressed as it should due to the government not reacting with productive measures to reverse climate change.

The question is as we introduce what will be covered in this book, it seems evident that with all the media portraying this climate warming, people don't realize how serious this issue is. The evidence is there about a future that will not be okay for our future generations as they try to cope or adapt to a planet this is too hot to sustain any form of stability. In the context of how past warm periods and cold periods did stabilize the trend of climate change with little effect. However, the current trend of warmth has being going on for 150 years now and has no signs of slowing down anytime soon. In fact, with the robotic age coming soon, as we watch movies like divergent and allegiant, this is how our world will be in 100 years. So, one can imagine how hot it will be in the 22nd century, not something that we desire to think about cause of the inability to process the damage our behaviors are causing.

One must realize how bad it can get before we finally realize that it is too late to change the course of history. In fact, it might already be too late to reverse the damage of greenhouse gases and CO2 emissions into the atmosphere. It is thus evident that we stop and look around at the state of the world and comprehend what exactly we are doing to this world. If everyone can see the changes that are happening, such a catastrophe can be avoided but this will never be the reality till this planet is exhausted. Thus, are there any other planets that can harbor life in our solar system beyond earth? Such a question is interesting cause scientists have tried to determine this but without any effect. Thus, mars or mercury may be good fits but then again, there could be aliens on both those planets.

You are probably wondering why this book is being written and the purpose of all this talk now in 2019 about climate change? The answer seems evident that we need to realize everything that is happening is due to man-made climate change. What this means is that it is not due to the natural affect of the earth warming up or going in these cycles of warm and cold periods which will be talked about in this book. It is more about our choices that we are making each day, week, month and year. If only people would stop and think about what they are doing when they litter on the street, or drive everywhere, then maybe the planet will be better off. However, people are so consumed in their own reality of self-fulfillment that they find even thinking about the future impossible.

To be honest it is scary thinking about climate change because it so real and getting to a point of no return. So, what determines a person's life, not caring seems evident and is shameful but we cannot force others to view the threat as real as it is. The contents of this book will be scary to read since it involves current and worsening threats that will in fact destroy this world. However, we must dive into the reality since our future depends solely on it. If we don't act now, then what will our future be like if the planet goes out the window. There are people very worried about climate change so much they are becoming activists for change. It seems to me, that others won't follow suite because they are not informed about what is really happening or they just don't care.

Why then should we care? Caring is the notion that as a world we have failed to adapt to changes in climate that will persist causing more new normal weather events. These events are already starting to happen around the globe and will get much worse till we have summer in winter. The reverse could be true to have winter in summer. It is such a change that society should care about the future and what it will look like because it will not get any better unless people realize this is only going to get worse.

Looking at the future seems like it is not going to be good for humans as the climate warms up, these extreme weather events continuing and becoming part of a new normal that will scratch any hope of a cool down, stay tuned for what is coming up in this book cause the time to act is now. If the climate warms at the rate it is currently going, then it will take an asteroid impact to cool the planet and end global warming.

CONTENTS

CHAPTER 1

Global warming is the reality of our poor choices that we continue to adapt and wont change regardless of what the experts tell us not to do. So, what really is this global warming and how does it influence how we make our choices regarding how to not take care of god created universe. Such a travesty indeed to think that this has never happened before, yes, we have had warm and cool period including a ice age lasting basically 350-400 years which will be talked about later but for now is what is the fuss all about.

The definition is long and has lots of parts but the 1st is changes to earth's climate or long-term weather patterns that vary from place to place. It could be snowing in July somewhere in the northern hemisphere where usually it is hot and sunny. Or it could be hitting the 20s in January in the same hemisphere when it is supposed to be cold and snowy. Such that these climate changes basically have the effect of the planet trying to stabilize any sort of level ground knowing everything is in chaos and there is nothing that can be done to destabilize the planet to level out the core temperature which is shifting constantly.

Climate change and global warming usually mean different things because global warming is just warming while climate change is the whole puzzle that seems to have too many pieces that either wont fit or cannot endure the complexity of what the reality is regarding human caused disaster. Such a change is the notion that some places will always remain cold due to their location around the globe. Such these places never really heat up in the summer and yet in the winter it is so cold. However even with snow in the summer is normal in such places because it is so north. The notion then is why different countries are warmer than others or colder than others seems like a question that has no reason to discover. With, it is potent that we know that climate change is more than just weather, but the whole picture of a complex system of systems that are becoming erratic due to human caused man-made fossil fuels and greenhouse gases.

Winter is usually milder than it has ever been due to climate change which stems from the inability for the earths surface to cool due to the sun becoming increasingly stronger and blocking any coldness that the atmosphere wants to engage due to those gases being trapped into the upper atmosphere. Thus, it is possible for it to be 20.c in February in France, yet Alberta is -35. C. This is normal for the parts of this hemisphere with the location and the notion of deserts that lie within each surface of the earth.

Climate changes also involves more extreme weather events that are not normal and are of a concern like extended cold snaps in the winter. These cold snaps basically don't break up after a few weeks but persist for 3 months. North America in 2019 had their worst arctic outbreak from Feb 3- Mar 10 which was the nastiest even seen. However, something that wasn't forecasted happened due to climate change. Yet people say well global warming causes it to be warmer so the extended cold must be due to an ice age or global cooling. Well, that is not correct cause how can the planet be cooling if we are each year placing in the top 10 for warmest years, and months on record.

If the planet was cooling, it would be evident everywhere even in places that are normally very hot like Mexico. However, that is not occurring because global cooling has not happened since February 1984 which was the last month globally that was colder than normal. Such a trend is the reality that global warming will continue each month even though some places are colder than normal even record cold, others will be record breaking heat. That is true climate change due to man-made poor choices to continue with all the destruction of the earth.

Global warming is more importantly some serious climate variations that aren't going to be redirected to the point they were before. As we have seen, the topic of what is climate change stems from all the stories of extreme weather events encompassing the globe that don't seem to even break. If the planet was to revert to what it was when god created it, then global warming didn't exist because Jesus was in control of the globe and how hot and cold it will be. We have not listened to god and went our own way of doing things which stem from our inability to listen to the scientists and experts that state it will get worse. Look around you, the weather we had this year in BC, drought and fire, cold snaps lasting 1 month, more extreme weather destroying the globe, are you scared yet.

The fact that humans aren't concerned for the climate and planet worries me since it seems that the world is tuned into how much money or possessions, they can obtain rather than protecting the earth and stewarding what god made in his perfect image. Why would you destroy Jesus's creation because of selfishness and egotism? People need to wake up and open their eyes look around and see the damage of the windstorm from last fall in BC, that will be a hurricane if we don't stop and change our behaviors.

Global warming is the extreme events that will occur every single year that eventually will change the temperature trends despite the Enso effect. This is the concern of a world that seems to not care about anything rather than living and polluting the globe instead of recycling and reusing what they have. Global warming isn't like the Enso effect that strange weather encompasses the world for 9-12 months then goes away and it stabilizes. Global warming doesn't end after 9-12 months, it continues to affect the climate for months on end till the

Jetstream changes and is diverted either north or in another direction changing the planet altitude of temperature.

The Enso effect is warm periods, cold periods, and neutral periods that are normally part of the climate shift. El Niño which BC is experiencing currently happens every 2-7 years and leads to warmer weather in BC with drier than normal precipitation which is the case so far in 2019 minus February. Global warming is the driver of El Nino events becoming longer and stronger due to the change in the earth climate. Such an effect cannot be comprehended due to the lack of understanding what is really going on. El Nino has been the driver in BC weather mostly in the last 5 years due to climate change although this 2019 event is weak but is lasting longer than usually due to climate change. Weak El Nino events last 6 months then end, but so far, the 2019 event shows no signs of abating anytime soon. In fact, this Weak El Nino should become moderate and last into 2020. The reality then is can we prevent El Nino from lasting this long? Nope it doesn't seem possible because of the notion of the climate shifting to a warmer period that wont lead to an ice age for a long time. There will be cool periods like La Nina in the future but will be much weaker due to another feature which is the pacific decadal oscillation. This feature is currently in a positive phase meaning warmer weather will persist most El Nino till it changes into the colder phase where La Nina will rule.

Therefore, all the above are due to the topic of what is global warming because it encompasses everything from the PDO to the Enso effect and the extreme weather events that wont shift and end anytime soon.

Talking more about the PDO which is interesting because it is exactly why it has been so warm and dry in BC since 2014. The PDO is in a positive phase meaning that the climate is shifting to adapt to the inability for the Jetstream to stabilize which is not good. The PDO prior to 2014 was in a colder phase meaning those springs and summers weren't as hot and dry. Since 2000 up to 2014 the PDO has been in a negative phase except for July 2002- June 2006 and June 2009- May 2010. Other than those times, it was negative meaning the Gulf of Alaska wasn't as hot so early July some years were in the high teens and wet. Summer for a few years was only 2 months long due to La Nina and the cold effect of the PDO. Spring for like 5 years from 2008-2012 was cold and wet due to the negative climate shift with La Nina.

As we look back at those years the examiner must endure the reality that forest fires weren't a concern as summer was even wet at times. Now in 2019, and since 2014 it has been every year starting in early May it start to hit 20.C and doesn't end till early October. Even one year like 2017 it was 20.c at the end of October due to the heatwave that usually wouldn't produce such extreme weather spike at that time of the year. In fact, in years like 2011, it was below 10.c at the end of October due to both the negative PDO and La Nina. In fact, in November 2011 it was mostly in the single digits everyday for high temperatures even snowing later in the month. With the PDO in the positive phase, it is evident that our climate on the BC side has warmed and the question is willing the PDO remain positive for 20-30 years or will it be like 2002-2006 short lived.

The PDO is looking like it will not shift into the colder phase till 2034 at the earliest which will mean these hot summers in BC and early springs with late falls are forecast to continue every year. Winter will be milder and wetter, and El Nino will occur more often till the PDO shifts back into the colder phase. However, with climate change it won't matter if the PDO shifts because the whole globe is out of sync.

Then, if we know that this is happening, the next question is what we will do when it is too hot to sustain life and the rivers are out of water. Then will we finally open our eyes and scream what its worth that our globe is destroying before our very eyes and we caused it to happen with selfishness and arrogance. Such changes need to be made and know we know all about warming.

CHAPTER 2

The main causes of global warming are to what extent a major implication for the reality that humanity is really messed up. Such that each time we hear about the causes of extended summer seasons and bitterly cold winters we wonder is this due to climate change. It isn't climate variability due to the notion that when the climate is variable it always reverts to the stabilizing balance. However, the reality is that it has nothing to do with the factors that we all think are accurate based on what the climate was in the past. It is like we have messed up the atmosphere so much that anything to reverse the effects seem pointless.

The first is water vapor which seems like blocking the clouds from cooling the climate. IE this year alone BC has experienced the humidex every day this summer and even not cooling below 20.C till 3 in the morning. How water vapor works is a magnificent reality that usually the sun cannot penetrate forever, and eventually the clouds move back in and cool things down. It seems evident only in desert areas that the sun can potentially block out the clouds because that is typical for that kind of climate.

Clouds and precipitation result in the temperature dropping due to the reality that the sun cannot penetrate through due to the thickness of the clouds. However, most of the time temperate climates have increased precipitation in the fall and winter seasons due to the natural effect of the time of the year. With that being stated, it seems evident that somehow, we have messed up that notion of the atmosphere preventing the sun from shining each day. What we have done is simply by emitting those gases into the atmosphere prevented the normal precipitation to occur in places that are aren't desert. It is normal for Arizona to never experience rain since that is normal cause there is no grass and it gets hot in the summer like over 40.C but in other places of Canada not so much. Yes, the interior of BC hits 30.C mostly in the summer because it is kind of a desert. However other places like Vancouver Island rarely see days above 30.C in the summer due to the mountain influence diverting that hot air away from the coast.

Water vapor is interesting since it explores what happens in the fall for example when the days start cooling down in the mornings. Dew is formed when the temperature goes below 10.C at night which usually starts happening in BC like late September. In fact, it is interesting to note why the leaves change color in the fall and shed all their foliage. It is since the water vapor is evident in these seasons due to the reality of the change from summer into fall.

During the fall we usually get fog due to the water vapor settling in overnight in many areas as the temperature is usually cooling down low enough for the air to form crystals that magnify everything great about the fall season. In the fall, at night t shirt attire is usually not evident since it is too cold to even entertain that prospect. However, come November is when the first frost occurs means the temperature hits 0.C. Usually this time of the year is when the atmosphere is cooling down to the point that winter is on the horizon. Remember summer is only 3 months of the year and when it ends, it starts to cool right of. Mid-September is when the change happens as that is when the days are equal in day and night duration of 12 hours. It is evident that water vapor is never present in the summer only in the fall-spring. The only time water vapor is present in the summer is when it rains, and the temperature is between 10-15. C. Other than that, it mostly is warm enough to wear a t shirt.

How does water vapor point to climate change is the question since usually there is no answer? Mostly, the theory is that the more vapor is trapped in the stratosphere, the higher likely that the clouds will not form to block out the suns heat. Whereas if the sun is not being challenged by the vapor, then it is safe to state that humans are the result of the consistent change in the vapor of water particles that are trapped into the atmosphere. For example, it is not normal in October for it to be 17.C-20.C at 9pm because the sunset is 6:30pm. The reality is one would assume it would cool down when the sun sets behind the clouds and usually this is the case. However, if the water vapor is not doing what it should, then the atmosphere cannot cool properly and thus leads to the temperature not moving.

Second is Co2 or carbon dioxide and this has a major effect of the current cause of climate change. The reason CO2 is released is mostly due to volcanic eruptions around the world. These events happen all the time and it releases the lava into the atmosphere which in turn causes the heat to be trapped in the ozone. Thus, if the toxic substance of lava is bad enough, the fact that the CO2 is released means that the vapor is not dealing with the issue and as a result the planet heats. However, there have been eruptions that have caused ice ages, but this happened only in the 1600s.

CO2 is common and is all around us, we breath it in everyday, it is in our drinks and foods. It also is hidden in many items that one would think don't possess CO2 which is scary science, but it is relevant to the day and age. However, it is the emissions from vehicles that causes the most problems with CO2 because that way releases most of the issues into the atmosphere. It happens directly because cars emit so much gases and fumes due to the engine driving down the streets. The more people drive, the more CO2 is released into the atmosphere and this causes the planet to warm because the vapor is not enough to replace the incoming overload of CO2 emitted from the vehicles.

It is the reality that CO2 alone causes most of the man-made global warming because it is intentional. People intentionally drive for no reason and this causes the atmosphere to become polluted since humanity is all about self-destruction than self-preservation. Why would people intentionally desire to destroy the planet? They don't realize that CO2 will cause the atmosphere to have trapped gases that in turn will cause climate change to continue to get worse until we end up hotter than mars. Think about how many cars are on the road today, way too many and this is problematic because if you need to drive to work fine, but for no purpose just stop and ditch it.

Deforestation is another way CO2 is released into the air and this is problematic because people enjoy cutting down trees. If the tree is dying and this is okay but if the tree is perfectly healthy then it shouldn't have to be cut down. People don't realize that their actions of destroying nature will lead to climate change but again humanity is foolish. How could someone cut down a tree that has birds and other species in it, those humans are not only putting the climate at risk, they are putting species at risk. It is so selfish and foolish that people would not consider other species that have to survive their home being chopped down because of someone who desires to make money.

Burning fossil fuels is another way CO2 is trapped into the earth and this is mostly from fires heated homes. If someone has a wood stove fire every night in the fall and winter, then basically the smoke is released into the atmosphere causing the climate to change. However, people don't realize how serious it really is because the thought process is distorted. If you keep using a gas wood stove, then the emissions will lead to climate to change, how silly is this. For me, my parents used a gas wood stove fire and it was contained with no issues, but people burn leaves and other trash that doesn't need to be burned.

Fossil fuels from other sources lead to issues but usually aren't as bad as smoke because they are in lower concentrations. However, we need to realize that if humanity is behind the production of these fossil fuels, then it is safe to say that people don't know how to do anything correct to save a planet that is already messed up because of these fossil fuels burning and this is the reality of a planet that is ready to react in a negative way. The factories that make paper need to know how to do it safely so that no emissions are released into the atmosphere and this will replace anything that people deem to be relevant cause they are stupid anyway.

The issue is that CO2 is the main cause of global warming because it has been going on since way back. People don't realize that this is the reason our climate is changing, and the patterns of weather are becoming more erratic. However as stated humans will not change their ways ever because it is like they don't think about the future generations that will have to clean up the mess of the past.

Methane is another cause of climate change and this one is often overlooked due to the notion that it is usually off the radar. However, agriculture activities use this gas to grow their crops and livestock. Usually the cause of climate change is related to whether the producer of the agricultural land uses the fertilizer in the right way. However, as we can see, most of the time it is safely consumed to the land that the farmer is planting on.

Landfill waste is a reason for methane being released into the atmosphere due to the reality that once the garbage gets into the landfill it only takes not much effort to pollute the planet. Usually if some company throws everything in the landfill instead of recycling it, then the methane is released into the atmosphere which causes the planet to suffer the consequences. Whatever we put in the landfill will have negative consequences if the behavior is not changed or altered.

Society must realize that in order to preserve what we have left of this planet, then we should stop using landfills to dispose of all our garbage.

Now manure management with domestic livestock is another example of methane being released into the atmosphere. This way is obvious in rural areas such that the main source of income and production is from farms and livestock. However, noted that the reality of people thinking that in these small areas, it is safer to produce the livestock and manure necessary to keep the farms going. When in doubt, a farmer must realize that their best efforts to curb the effects of what methane is produced as a result of their choices has costs to the planet. Usually it is scuffed as no big deal because it is just manure, but this is a result of the planet responding to various levels of this gas in excess to the reality of how much is needed.

Methane from farts is not very important because it is from a human being. However, as we can see, this sort of methane still contributes to climate change because if we do it on the street, the gas from our body will release into the air traveling upward. It is accurate to assume that humanity is constantly releasing methane from their bodies each day causing probably lots of gas to be accumulated into the air. With methane being a gas that stinks in the form of fart, it is safe to say that humans release a lot of it.

Nitrous oxide is another form of gas that can cause global warming. Usually this is known as laughing gas meaning it is odorless and can knock someone out. If you ever got your wisdom teeth out, the dentist injects a sedative that has the oxide in it, and it causes the brain to shut off causing sleep. It is usually for the duration of the procedure to prevent the sufferer from experiencing any pain while the teeth are extracted.

Usually this form of nitrous oxide really doesn't pollute the planet because it is not released into the air, but into the person. However, there are other man-made environmental causes of this gas that will contribute to the warming of the planet. Through soil cultivation practices, it is possible to produce enough of this gas to really mess up the planet. People think that soil cannot possibly do anything to harm the environment but that thinking is flawed since it is what we do with soil that is the issue. If soil is used to make things, then the process of cultivating it will indeed lead to negative climatic effects.

Mostly the fertilizer to kill anything like weeds and produce fruit in the growing season is the cause of the gas emitting into the air. Besides killing weeds, fertilizer helps plants grow and trees stay alive, so it is very important but dangerous cause it emits the oxide which effects the climate. People need to understand using fertilizer has its ups and downs because if the planet cannot take a lot of the chemicals, then the air will be polluted. Plus, the toxicity of the fertilizer on human health causing long term health issues.

CFCs mostly used in industrial occupations are considered greenhouse gases because they contain things to pollute the air. In construction and other occupations that emit these harmful chemicals into the air, it is safe to assume that the negative effects are far binding. As people don't realize that welding or smelting and other occupations that rely of the CFC to achieve the effect of the product being finished can have negative effects on the atmosphere. People need to understand that their jobs that they engage in might not only put their health at risk, it will most certain put the climate at risk.

The solution is instead of emitting these chemicals, emit something else that is safer for the environment meaning less gas is produced into the air. Mostly people need to realize that in order to curb any effects of these chemicals being emitted starts with knowledge. This knowledge comes from the person who makes the products that will use the chemicals in order to make them work. Such that if the producer knows of the risks, they can better access how to prevent a situation that will pollute the air.

This has been around for hundreds of years and is why we see all the buildings and roads. It was the industrial revolution that produced the concrete and wood that inhabits people to live and drive on. However, it must be noted that in order to stop or reduce climate, change starts with knowledge of what the risks are of ignoring the trials of how we shouldn't go about doing or creating our things.

If the ozone layer can be destroyed by these chemicals, then it will never get its stability back. This will lead to more intense climatic effects that will cause the destruction of the planet and species in it. Such effects will be catastrophic to all species and the future generations because of all the gases that are emitted into the air every day. Changes need to be made to preserve what we have left.

The main causes of climate change are the reality of a society that has not done things right. The basis of why we keep doing the things to pollute and destroy the environment is beyond reasoning. It mostly states how a society full of people who don't care about anything other than money can ever comprehend what the future effects will be. If people are this ignorant and selfish now, what will it be like when robots take over in 100 years. Eventually this planet will be so hot it will not be able to sustain any life or species. Wondering this causes most to consider why they even bother making a difference to stop global warming when most people continue directly destroying the planet god created.

It takes courage to face the reality of a fallen system of choices that directly impact the core of the planet. What will it take for us to wake up and realize global warming is not going away until we address the causes of all the gases that contribute to the demise of this planet? How hot does it have to get so people realize how screwed up it is. Or will it not make any difference if it is 20.C in the winter every year in regions such as west coast of Canada. The goal is to look around and see the destruction and think do I want this for my future generations.

CHAPTER 3

Hurricanes are a powerful force of nature that are both scary and interesting at the same time for storm chasers who love nature at its finest. The reality that hurricanes occur each year strikes the most comparison to the reality that all it takes is the pressure to be released to create such a cataclysm. Most of the hurricanes occur in the Atlantic Ocean and are in the category 1-5 range with some tropical storms, this chapter will touch on the various categories of hurricanes.

Starting with why hurricanes occur is the reality of fascination into the temperament of mother nature. How can mother nature be so angry all the time when she must take a chill pill but that is not the way she desires to act. With such knowledge into why she acts in such a manner paints a picture that our world is screaming at us to change our ways. The planet is letting the 7.5 billion people realize how their current actions impact the climate and mood of mother nature.

When mother nature is angry, she states it with such clarity and passion it is evident trouble brews on the horizon. She must be angry enough to let the while world know each year by intensifying the hurricanes/cyclones that cause millions of dollars in damage. However, it must be noted that mother nature has no mercy for witless, idiotic people that choose to keep destroying her habitat. She clearly has no obligation to stop anytime soon, but to keep going until the world is destroyed by damage caused by her hurricanes.

Before we dive into the 5 categories of hurricanes it must be stated that the reader must realize the reality of a changing planet. If the person notes that each time, they think their neck of the woods is safe, it must be asserted that it isn't always the case. If people don't think about what effects climate change has on the earth, then it is obvious the notion of fearing mother nature isn't evident.

People think that El Nino brings less hurricanes then Enso Neutral and La Nina. That thinking is partly correct but, nothing can really prevent the water from heating to the point that hurricanes happen. The warmer climate has a lot to do with how many intense hurricanes will hit each year and the strength of each one. If we keep polluting and destroying our gracious planet, then it seems evident that major hurricanes will occur in places that aren't custom to such travesties like the west coast of north America.

Why would hurricanes occur in North America near the pacific northwest? It sounds impossible to assume that we can have hurricanes if the mountains protect us from most of the damaging storms. However, as noted climate change will find a way to counterbalance any attempt for the atmosphere to destabilize to the point where it will be evident that these hurricanes will hit Victoria BC. Scary thinking when it doesn't seem real but in nature anything is possible to occur, and the screwed-up logic is thinking it won't happen which is plain ignorance.

Hurricanes not only increase due to climate change; they occur more frequently and cause more damage than those mini tropical storms that tend to hit BC in fall and winter. These monster windstorms are destruction and scary with the driving rains, like heavy and winds that would toss someone 10 feet in the air if ventured outdoors in peak gusts.

Every single hurricane is defined by the severity of how long they last and most lasting up to 3 days. Such events can traumatize people who witness homes being ruined and trees falling everywhere. Thankfully BC isn't in the neck of the woods regarding hurricanes because even the west coast has experienced hurricane force winds with nasty winter storms. Such like in 2018 on Dec 20 when 100kmh winds rippled through the island of Vancouver causing major power outages and leaving branches everywhere.

BC might be avoiding of the nasty hurricanes, but one year back in 2006 in mid-December, a hurricane form windstorm hit Stanley park in Vancouver BC destroying everything in its path and causing lots of damage. Those that witnessed that storm call it one for the century books as it was a very intense freak of nature. However, those storms will increase due to climate change which seems scary, but it is relevant for our day.

In fact, a report in 2012 stated that BC will experience hurricanes one day due to climate change, so the western part of the world isn't immune to the powerful effects of mother nature and its vices. Thus, it seems evident that humanity is not ready for the events that will follow if mother nature increases her wrath and spreads it to the western part of North America. Hopefully she doesn't come to the brink where she must cause such agony, but her patience is wearing thin. She must believe that humans won't protect her and thus she demands revenge against everyone that is polluting her.

So, what defines a category 1 hurricane? A category 1 hurricane is defined as a system that produces winds from 119-153 kilometers per hour. We use kilometers per hour because that is how Canada measures windspeed. The winds are very dangerous in that the sound of the gusts are enough to get one very scared. Personally, BC has never experienced such a windstorm, but we have had serious close calls. The likelihood of a hurricane 1 strength hitting BC is slim, but it is best to be prepared.

The damage caused by such hurricanes could be some destruction to roofs of houses and buildings but not enough for the roof to cave in. Siding and gutters will have damage to them as a result of the wind. As well as large branches, off trees will snap causing damage to nearby houses and buildings. Shallow rooted trees that are not very strong will be toppled and on their side.

As a result of the wind, damage to power lines and poles will cause power outages lasting 2-3 days. This means it is best to have an emergency kit ready to go, that will last you 3 days. It is wise you put things inside it like water, food mostly bland, cleaning supplies, toothpaste, money, clothes and anything that will last you 3 days. With the power being out, you may be without TV or internet for days, thus a radio will come in handy.

BC has never seen these hurricanes but due to a warming planet, it is likely that in the next 10-20 years, the west coast could start having these types of systems during summer months. How scary would it be to see wind gusts as strong as 119-153 kph, that is freaky and will be for anyone who is looking out their window when the peak wind gusts are happening. The driving rain which will be torrential, and those high winds will likely cause chaos in the person and time to head for the basement.

Category 2 hurricane is the next level up and with this is more extreme in terms of gusts and damage. The kph with this range is 154-177 meaning the gusts are extreme and nastier which will cause lots of damage more than a category 1. The roofs of well-constructed homes will suffer major damage to the roof, siding and gutters. The shallow trees will be completely uprooted and even land onto roads blocking traffic. Near total power loss meaning everywhere without power will last from several days to several weeks. This means for up to 3 weeks without any power.

Category 3 hurricane with wind speeds of 178-208 kph is a major system that will be more dangerous than the first two. The phase devastating damage is the notion that at this level is hard to imagine how much destruction will occur. The roof of constructed homes will be taken right off meaning if you were inside the home you could see the sky. Many trees even those that are higher up and stronger will be snapped blocking roads and leaving destruction in their wake as toppling down.

Both electricity and water will be not available for up to 3 weeks after the storm meaning if someone would desire to take a bath or drink water, it would be tough without water. Without electricity on top of that would be utter misery, it would be impossible to make it without both and thus homelessness is the only answer. However, just the thought of being homeless for 3 weeks sounds basically scary.

Category 4 hurricane is getting up their and is much scarier with gusts of 209-251 kph and this is almost a tornado. The phase catastrophic damage will occur seems like it is almost habitual to assume that it will be a war zone. The loss of roof and even walls of houses will be damaged to a great extent and the picture is more consistent with a major earthquake than a hurricane. Trees snapped and power lines down will cause a seen of mess. Power could be out for months due to the damage to poles and the area will not be able to sustain humans for a time afterwards. Just the picture of this type of hurricane is scary to think about cause if you watched movies, you would see what the reality is, and by god it is frightful.

Category 5 is the final and most destructive type of hurricane and thus is considered at tornado because it is so strong and devastating. Gusts of 252kph and higher defines this type of storm and therefore is a tornado. If you watched the wizard of oz, that storm was a type 5 hurricane that thrust Dorothy into the sky where she landed in another dimension. Most homes will be destroyed meaning they would have to be rebuilt. This would cost a lot of money to restore a home that has been destroyed but a hurricane of this strength. It is scary to think that these types of systems can occur, but with the right energy and speed, it is possible.

The same as type 4 regarding power failure and area being not occupied, the seriousness of such a storm makes one ponder how could mother nature be so cruel? She is cruel because she is sick and tired of ignorant people destroying her habitat and beauty. If she must create nasty hurricanes to wake the world up, then so be it. It is evident then that humanity is not aware of these disasters till they happen. Most people don't think twice about the notion that if their behavior continues, it will lead to the earth destroying itself.

The final thought is the reality that hurricanes are a force of nature and thus cannot be stopped or prevented. With the right temperature of water and conditions, these monster storms will wreak havoc on the USA causing millions of dollars in damage until the world wakes up and sees what their actions are taking. The notion that humans don't know how to prepare for these events tells the picture of ignorance and plain boredom in the face of such adversity. However, people must note their efforts to curb a reality that will be destructive for their future generations and thus is the point of recognition. In order to stop mother nature from unleashing her fury is to stop causing her distress.

CHAPTER 4

The topic of heatwaves and droughts regarding climate change seem relevant to discuss knowing the reality of how heat can trigger things. Heatwaves happen usually in the summer and no other time of the year due to the sun being at its highest during June-August. However, in recent decades heatwaves have occurred in all seasons including the usually cold winter. This has been noted in various parts of the world and in fact even north of the equator. Whereas true heatwaves can occur in spring-summer common due to the sun being high.

In BC heatwaves have occurred as early as march and in 2019, the BC coast had a mini wave of hot temperatures for 4 days which is abnormal considering usually BC at that time is wet and cold. However, after a brutal winter that featured lots of snow and cold snaps, it shifted right into summer heat which is abnormal even for that part of the world. Heatwaves light the ones we had in BC during the 2018 summer season were enormous and even disastrous if you consider the many heat warnings posted for BC during that summer. The heatwaves have occurred every single summer and have been very intense noting that the reality of trying to sleep at night and walk during the day seems almost impossible.

However, one would suspect that after September there would be no more heat spikes in BC due to the natural cooling of the sun at that time of the year in BC. The reality that in October 2017 we had in BC 2-4 days of 20.c or above in late October which is the latest heatwave ever recorded in BC. Never has a heatwave occurred after early October and this is the situation of climate change and its extremes. However, we have gotten up to 28.c in early October in the Cowichan

Valley which is natural for the beginning of October but after the mid part of the month, it never really hits even 15.c so the rarity of the heatwave at that point of the year points a concern that only designates with a warming world.

BC or even western Canada have never experienced heatwaves between late October and early march due to the cooling of the sun preventing that spike in temperature which is typical for that period of the year. However, due to climate change, the reality of more extreme weather events leading up to nastier heatwaves at times when normally it is cold and wet seem evident that our world is increasing in temperature. Just imagine what would occur if it reached 20.c for 5 days in February or even January. This seems rare for BC as it never gets above 10.c many days in December and January, however as noted climate change is behind the increasing heatwaves that have ravaged the globe.

The effects of heatwaves are heat stroke and exhaustion which is consistent with the humidex making it feel even hotter than it really is. The problem is usually during the summer many people are outdoors enjoying the nice weather but too few realize that heat illness is very common at that time of the year. Such that an experience like heat sickness can trigger with it the notion that something is wrong if it is so hot that humans are getting ill. I know people that have had heat illness and is not fun as well as sunburns which combined would make someone feel very sick like they have the flu.

Most of the world's population lives in hot areas which create lots of heat related illnesses, and the higher temperature, the more likely of a sickness. To give an example of what types of illnesses would occur when it gets above 30.c, the list is cholera, and other diarrhea illnesses like parasites and food poisoning, malaria due to increase in mosquitos. As well as dengue fever and other illness such as the sleeping sickness with the tee fly.

Such illnesses are due to the natural increase in temperature and the body increasing to adapt to the rising pressure on the human. Therefore, it is natural to state that even in BC when it gets above 20.c for a period, diarrhea and illnesses in that category become commonplace. Therefore, that is why intestinal illnesses of bacterial and parasitic nature are more common in hot summer months than cooler winter months. Norovirus is common in winter and thus never has many outbreaks in hot summer months because it is resistant to the heat, it thrives more in cool conditions.

The lucky reality is that Canada doesn't have to endure these illnesses the other world suffers because the treatment of medicine is better in detecting vaccinations for all these illnesses that would cause lots of distress among the citizens. As well as we have great doctors and nurses in Canada that can treat these conditions before they become bad. That isn't to say that Canadians don't suffer from infections in summer because it isn't as hot, it is common due to the heat being in the atmosphere every day.

Even agriculture and produce takes a hit when it is too hot, in fact too much heat can cause produce to become too ripe and melt away. Take the farms that rely on water to fertilize their crops, if it doesn't rain then those crops dry out and will not endure the great harvest in the fall. Although some produce does very well in the heat but in places of desert like Arizona, farmers cannot grow much produce due to it being way too hot.

However, it must be noted that even trees suffer from extreme dry hot spells and the leaves turn color earlier than usual due to the reality of lack of precipitation. Trees in BC need water to stay the lush green color that points to summer and a healthy tree due to the rain. In desert areas, due to lack of precipitation, the trees aren't having leaves on them because it gets way too hot and therefore there aren't and grass areas just desert.

Drought is another concern of climate change and is related to heatwaves but is much more common and long lasting. Every year in BC for the last 5 has been a major drought, 2019 being the worst on record. The winter was very dry, spring was very dry, summer was dry although wasn't as dry as in recent years. However, we have had worse droughts than ever before due to climate change and a warming planet. In fact, every year in BC it is expected to be very dry for spring-fall.

This is a concern because in 2019, the Cowichan Valley almost ran out of water due to the record low river levels. Stage 4 drought was issued and thus the weir had to be pumped with water from emergency sources just to keep it afloat. However, as stated BC has had this issue for a long time and shows no signs of letting up. Even if BC has a wet winter, spring-fall being drier than normal will cause lots of spells without rain which will be devastating in the long term. The snowpack is weaker every year due to milder winters that seem to only be getting milder. Thus, if climate change doesn't stop which shows no signs of, then these droughts will occur year-round even in the winter.

Droughts can have nasty impacts on the forests and create forest fires that ravage land and burn hectares. Such BC has experienced many bad forest fire seasons, take 2017 and 2018 which were the two worst forest fire seasons on record with the most fires and hectares burned. It is scary to note that these events are becoming every year reality but that is climate change for you, a warming planet fueling more extreme long-lasting weather events such as droughts causing fires. In fact, BC in 2019 didn't have such a bad forest fire season due to wet summer and lots of rain in July and August. However, don't count on that continuing every year because climate change will cause more forest fire seasons causing massive fires and droughts.

Droughts can destroy hectares and threaten homes that are in the wake of the flames. For example, Slave Lake in Alberta June 2017 had massive forest fires that destroyed the whole town causing major displacement and lots of dollars of damage. The reality of climate change and a warming world is evident that these events will get more extreme and frequent occurring all year. It may be wetter in the fall-winter, but in due time all year will be drought and fires. Although, October-March forest fires don't happen because it isn't hot and dry, but climate change will quickly change that reality.

The likely of drought various with the reality of expecting very warm spring-fall and a wet winter which is normal for BC. In fact, winter has been cold and wet while the other 3 seasons have been hot and dry. Such a reality is knowing that water restrictions have started as early as April some years due to a very dry winter and spring leading to a nasty long summer of drought. Thus, these conditions will continue and get more intense there fore it is evident to look forward to when spring gets going to expect the drought to happen.

In recent years, BC has had bone dry brown grass as early as late April due to the dry conditions that are the result of a persistent ridge of high pressure that prevents and moisture to lead the breakdown causing the climate to stabilize. Thus, due to the blob of 2014-2016 caused massive drought and fire in BC during that period, it is evident of it continuing. We have another blob like that one started in summer 2019 and is strengthening as we speak rival the last one. Therefore 2020 and the next 5 years in BC will be bad drought, fire and heatwaves due to the blob and the effects of any El Nino events that occur in that period.

It is not just BC; it is the whole world that is suffering through these droughts and heatwaves some places reaching 50.c in summer. The reality of a warming planet that will continue to warm causes great concern in the notion that humanity is not waiving the changes as suspicious, they are not caring about the effects due to both lack of respect and stupidity. Both can cause one to think about how it could come to this. How could mother nature be getting so hot and letting us feel her wrath? Why does she want to cause this much suffering and dry us out?

The answers to the above questions seem evident that it is not about how she does it, it is more why she is doing it. She doesn't want us to feel at ease with all the effects of heatwaves on the planet, she wants us to think about the future and how bad it will get and trust me, no one wants to know. Such a reality seems scary for those that don't know anything about why it is so hot because they live in a part of the world that never gets above 20.c. However, even those people must realize why this is happening and to what extent will they do anything about it. It seems that a society that is about wasting and self-destruction realizes the pity in it all because they don't seem to mind causing mother nature to become mad.

She has had enough, so she has set the fire and will not led up until this planet is too hot that she will make sure it is not going to be nice to those that disobey her and everything she wants to do with it. The hotter and drier it gets, the most likely of more disasters and sickness leading to the extinction of many species that are already suffering due to a warming world. Spring-summer being the hottest 6 months of the year is due to the reality that humanity is knowingly not creating with it such adverse conditions with all the hype about what we should do to keep cool in the summer. It is evident that these droughts and heatwaves will increase and become common even in places that aren't accustom to such events such as Iceland.

Such places that don't experience heat because they are way north of the equator are even hitting 20.c which is rare for places that high up but it is climate change that is impacting the melting of arctic ice that will lead to more warmer seas. It is the ice that keeps the water cooler and if there is not enough ice to cool the water, then the heat is trapped in the ocean causing with it more heatwaves and droughts.

Also, the Jetstream is to blame but is not all that of an issue due to the notion that climate change has been going on since the first warm period. Yeah there have been warm and cool periods in this world, but the ice age has always followed a nasty warm period. The question is how hot is enough? Will it have to reach 60.c in certain parts of the world in summer months for people to finally take mother nature seriously? Or will it even matter because it doesn't scare anyone, oh its hots every year what is the big deal right? This is wrong thinking because it is not so much how hot it gets, but for how long and how extreme the heat events are. Time to adapt to the new normal because these droughts and heatwaves will occur every spring lasting into the fall, so get ready world mother nature is about to turn up the dial.

CHAPTER 5

Winter outbreaks with cold snaps are the next focus in the reality of climate change and this is more of a concern. Every year we always get cold snaps in the winter and snowstorms as this is the natural way that winter shows itself in north part of the globe. We can even have up to 30cm of snow in one sitting as it is typical at this time of the year with the colder air and moisture being trapped in a cycle of the water temperature. BC has experienced many snowstorms every year and the key with this mild climate is that the snow never sticks around. The rain comes and melts it away however in 2019 that didn't happen like it usually would.

However, on February 3, 2019 after a mild 2/3 of winter in BC that featured no snow on the coast and very balmy temperatures, winter showed herself with a vengeance. It was the worst February on record for snow, the coast of BC saw more snow in this month than during the whole previous winter season. In 2018, BC despite a weak La Nina didn't experience as much snow, yeah, we had some in December around Christmas and February to a bit, but not as bad as 2019. The snow was so bad, the streets quite literally were blocked, and no one could walk anywhere without struggling just to make it across town.

Usually I go for evening walks around town at night but couldn't do this for 10 days because the snow was so high like 1 ½ feet. I never have seen this snow before in late winter, usually February is a month that in BC it is spring-like and flowers bulb everywhere. But, in 2019 the winter came in with such cruelty in what was a weak El Nino event. Usually El Nino doesn't produce as nasty snowfalls as other climate events. It was strange that in 2019 despite El Nino, it was so cold and snowy.

It wasn't just the snow that made headlines, it was the arctic system, the overnight lows being below 0.c for 3 weeks nonstop. It is normal to have it down to -2 and clear sky but during the say rising to 12.c in late February but -13 isn't normal. This happened on February 10th just before a massive snowstorm hit the valley. The snow from the previous week had almost melted and it looked like the pattern would break, but 35 cm of snow pummeled the region causing power outages and blockage of roads, no one was out driving or walking. For a Sunday night that is typical but usually there are more drivers even at night.

Schools were closed Monday-Wednesday and most businesses were shut down for 3 days including doctors offices. I never have seen in February such a cold snap and snow event that witnessed in 2019. It usually is mild and wet, and the rain comes in droves. It made sense that a mild climate for BC was put aside by an arctic high that wouldn't break until mid-March. During the February wicked winter snow and cold event, numerous records were broken and the usual late winter nice scenery of trees bulbing with flowers, golfers at the driving range and courses plus the early arrival of spring gear was non-existent. Winter is never longer land 2 weeks in BC due to a mild pacific flow of air which never occurred in 2019. We had it for the December-January period, but February wasn't typical.

Canada wasn't spared and it was worse due to a polar vortex while the other half of the northern hemisphere and the USA were very mild. It just hammered Canada and BC the arctic event which was the worst in history even nastier than the blizzard of 96. That year 100 cm of snow fell on Vancouver Island over 3 days causing roads to be blocked, power out and numerous stranded people that couldn't even leave their homes. This blizzard was followed by 100+ mm of rain that melted the snow and led to milder winter conditions for the rest of the season.

However, there was a milder system on February 15th that tried to break the arctic event apart and while it seemed it worked, the milder air wasn't strong enough to melt all the snow and lead to an early spring. Usually after 2 weeks of a nasty cold snap, the milder air comes in and rains crazy and snow melts in a week leading to consistent nice warm conditions because the Jetstream shifts back to the usual mild pattern. This never happened in 2019, instead the arctic air hung around for 1 ¼ months. It finally broke in early March when the temperature reached 10.c on March 12.

The result of a Jetstream that was stagnant meaning it didn't move for over a month tells a picture of climate change and even in March after the cold snap had ended, it was dry. Usually march is very wet and mild, it rains a lot in March. Parts of BC in this month exceed 150mm of rain at times because it is a wet month as a transition from winter into spring. Early spring in BC is always very wet due to the natural Jetstream shift but in 2019, the Jetstream favored the cool dry pattern which isn't usual. Usually it is mild and wet, and it rains a lot even into early April before drier conditions start in late April continuing into mid-September.

Winter in BC during the 2019 year was very dry like the driest ever seen and that was partly due to a weak El Nino but more of a stagnant arctic system that didn't break up to let milder conditions in. It is funny how in recent years, these events have occurred every year like 2017-2019 each February in BC has featured snow on the coast and that is a record of back-to-back years. 2016 was the last year, BC didn't experience the white stuff in February which isn't atypical because snow occurs in February but never as much. Whatever snow falls in BC during the winter especially near the coast melts very quickly, so it was surprising how long it lasted in 2019. How could we go from a very mild 2/3 of winter to a wicked cold last 1/3? It was climate change diverting the Jetstream and keeping it stagnant. Ironically during the summer of 2019 BC saw almost recording break rain in July a month that is usually dry and hot.

Therefore, I moved to Vancouver Island due to the milder conditions in the winter, but I was surprised it was so bad and cold in 2019. Never before have I seen this much snow and cold in late winter, when it usually is spring-like, in fact here is some science for you guys, every year February we get a taste of spring meaning there are 5-10 days that get above 10.c. Spring is defined by the temperature between 10-19. C and it could go as high as 19. C in February which is not abnormal.

What is abnormal is the reality that Vancouver Island had 0 days above 10.c in February so that taste of spring never came. The reality of this seems a joke right, but it isn't it happened. The Jetstream was to blame for this, in fact February 1st was the warmest day of the whole month, and the record high temperature for this month for Duncan BC is 19.c. Quite the winter we had in BC during 2019 which is why the focus on climate change is so evident. It points to a troubled future of more extreme weather events and even 3 months of arctic air for BC all winter long. This seems scary that spring-fall will be mild, and winter will be very cold. Climate change is serious and needs to be addressed because this reality of what just stated above has the potential to cause lots of emotion.

Look at climates that winter never comes like the southern part of USA and middle east as well as other countries in the northern hemisphere like Mexico. These climates are summer all year around and this is due to the natural cycle of the cold arctic air doesn't impact places like this because they are so south of the equator, it seems evident that winter wouldn't come to these parts of the globe. However, it has snowed in Mexico before and make no mistake, it will again in the future if climate change diverts the Jetstream which it seems to do each year. No wonder why Canadians escape from their country and head south during the winter because it is so cold and snowy, in fact Canada is the coldest country in the world and that is no spoiler.

As a result, Canada bears the brunt of winter causing the most snow and cold everywhere except the 2 coasts, east and west where it is mild. It is the Alberta-Manitoba area that usually get the cold and snow to a crazy degree especially Colorado lows which cause lots of snow and snowsqualls. However, BC coast had snowsqualls in February due to the wicked snowstorm. It isn't typical to experience these events on the coast due to the mild influence of air, which isn't the notion that our planet is already screwed up by the reality of climate change at its finest.

With this being said, it is evident that each year is getting colder in the winter and is a sign of things to come in the future, it could be a new norm for BC to experience these colder winters every single year instead of the mild conditions the province and coast are used to. This sounds redundant but it is the truth that climate change is already starting to impact our seasons in BC leading to longer growing seasons and more extreme weather events in the winter like snow. It will only get worse, until we realize how much it will take to reverse everything on its head about the reality of a changing climate that only seems to get worse by the year.

I am used to mild winters in BC, in fact I cherish the hot conditions in the winter because come February a jacket is not needed, and I look forward to an early spring each year, but in 2019 this never happened and is very unusual knowing it is not typical for the pattern to be favoring a stagnant weather pattern that doesn't break up, I usually work in the winter doing landscaping, but in 2019 I had no work till end of March. The lack of work and snow removal being the only think we could do seemed evident that winter was not going to let up until the end of the season which is rare for BC to have snow all the way up to spring.

It is evident that the snowstorms are getting more intense in BC and this is due to climate change not the Enso cycle. Even during La Nina years, it can be very mild and wet, but despite an El Nino 2019 featured record breaking snow in a month that usually doesn't get any snow but lots of rain. Such a reality is the notion that as a society and global enterprise, must know exactly why these events are occurring every year and what will it take to ditch the car and carpool or bike to work. If 2019 was this bad, then what will it be like in 10 years, 20 years, but the experts say it will be milder and warmer in the winter which is true climate change. This means that BC will get fewer winters like it had in 2019 and more winters like it had in 2015 where it was 3.c above normal for the coast and double-digit weather with no snow.

Hence, just because we get more extreme snow events and cold snaps doesn't point to colder winters in BC, it points to more extreme events due to climate change, but the general attitude is milder weather in winter months. This is the reality that climate change is occurring and getting worse, but is not the end of discussion, it is the start of what we as a world need to prepare for especially considered the moisture in these systems is increasing with climate change. Climate change is getting to be a hot topic especially in the winter as people blame the Enso cycle for the snow and cold which is not entirely true, there are many other factors to consider like the Jetstream and wind cycles. The next chapter is even more interesting with the rain and windstorms BC gets every year. 2019 featured intense snowstorms like never seen before, however it doesn't mean it will occur every year.

Even with all the snow BC had in 2019, it was still the worst drought ever due to lack of rain which is a normality of the winter season. However, 2019 is just one year, or is a sequence of more extreme snow events in months like December but not sticking around a week. In this case the snow will be more intense and lead to more accumulation, but the rain will melt it away very quickly. Such a reality is what drives people to consider the prospect of moving to a place like Arizona where it doesn't snow, however it has snowed in Apache Junction before just outside of Phoenix. I have been to Phoenix in December and it has been 5-7.c as a daytime high in late December typical of what BC experiences at that time of the year. It has snowed in the Arizona area before and even as south as Florida has had snow.

Such a reality is the notion that no one is immune to the effects of climate change, it is felt all across the globe and is a signal that mother nature is furious and she will not stop until her message is displayed for all the see and hear. It is evident then that people desire to become more eco friendly about the way we recycle our trash and garbage, but most folks don't give a say about anything, they just continue with their own ways. It is such a sad notion that folk don't care too much about this planet, but more about themselves which is quite sad.

It is scary to think of snowstorms in places like Egypt and other middle East countries, but it is possible with climate change, remember anything is possible with the erratic Jetstream you never know what could happen, Mexico could be 5. C and snow in the winter so those Canadians travelling to this part of the world to avoid the snow will be surprised to see the same stuff ruin their winter getaway.

Such a reality that even Hawaii will get snow, and this is a cause for concern, right? These warm areas that aren't accustom to winter will experience it, plus the whole globe will experience winter which seems scary that the snowstorms could travel such a distance but will climate change anything is possible.

If these warm areas experience snow, what does that say about our planet? It states that our planet is reaping the effects of climate change and a warming globe that will only feature more extreme winter snow events leading to snow in places that aren't accustom to it. If this is the new norm for this world, then it is scary to adapt to but in time humans must realize it is the reality. This is not a dream, this is now reality, the future reality if people don't wake up and think that next winter will be milder because it won't be. In fact, next year could be wicked cold and snowy all the way up till spring which doesn't seem like golfing and hiking will be a thing to do until the weather warms up. If you are going to the Caribbean for a dream vacation and see colder temperature, be on the lookout for the reality of a future based on the reality of climate change rearing its ugly head, what will you do now? Time to adapt or be consumed by its fury.

CHAPTER 6

The next topic of intense rain/windstorms in BC and across the globe point a picture that this world is warming to the point that every single year, more extreme weather events will happen causing massive storms like never seen before. This is the reality of a planet that is overheated and will explode if we don't do something about these nasty storms.

Every year in fall-winter BC gets nasty rainstorms called the pineapple express which is a system coming up from Hawaii leading to heavy rain and very warm temperatures reaching the high teens in months like November. This is natural and occurs 3-4 times in the course of a year because BC is in the bullseye of all the nasty rainstorms at that time of the year because of the Jetstream shift. The Jetstream and weather patterns associated will be introduced in the next chapter but for now is focusing on rain and wind events that seem to be getting nastier by the year.

Such pineapple express events can cause rain up to 100mm in 2 days which causes major flooding and leading to landslides and numerous health risks like boil water advisory. It is such that each event raises the question that is it typical or is there something else at play. If we have these rain events every year, it is safe to say they are getting worse with climate change which is not very rosy if you consider the reality that these types of events are the result of human caused global warming.

The tropical air comes from the south leading to rise in temperature with the rain when usually when it rains in the fall, it cools. In the case of the November 2nd, 2018 pineapple express event that landed on the coast of BC, November 1st wasn't that warm but rose to 15.c at the evening hour with heavy rain. It stayed at 13.c overnight and eventually rose to 17.c the next day as it cleared up and the system went away. This is typical of the nature of these types of systems since they bring up warm tropical air for a brief period of the time, not lasting more than 2 days. The concern now is how long in the future will these events last up to a week leading to broken high temperature records in months November-March reaching 20.c with such events.

Another event of this magnitude came in November 2014 early in the month when we had a similar situation but with nasty winds, the rain came at night and next day was blustery winds to the extent that a power light snapped and landed on car, the whole island was out of power for 8 hours maybe more for isolated areas. It is such these events that happen every year and the concern is that they are getting worse with climate change which is a cause for alarm.

It is normal to have such events, but the frequency of these events points the reality of a world that is on fire and will stop at nothing until it destroys us. BC has not been sparred because every single year, starting in November lasting sometimes into April we get these nasty wind and rainstorms. A example of a nasty year was 2006 and as the memory of that year is in the back of minds of people who were on the Vancouver island during that period, I remember how bad it was and it is no joke, climate change is real and getting worse.

What made the 2006 event so dramatic was that the first 2/3 of fall September-October was nice and mild even hitting 20.c in October but then on November 2nd 2006, the pattern changed and it led to nasty wind and rainstorms till early January of the next year, that is 2 months of lots of damage and warnings that were issued every day in BC. Never has the later fall featured such extreme storms that came one after the other after what was a nice fall up to the 2nd of

November. As we recall that year and how bad it was, thankfully it hasn't been as cruel since but still is a cause that our planet is heating up and these events will become more common like every year. Such storms are scary to watch and observe leaving one with the sense of dread knowing that the damage and chaos will follow.

The most powerful storm was in mid-December that featured a hurricane force event that toppled Stanley park in Vancouver BC. The pictures of such an event raises the question, how could the winds get so strong? If the water in the winter is cooler, then why was the speeds so high? These questions raise the reality that there wasn't a single explanation or theory as to why this occurred, but it preluded recent minor storms in weeks before that led to the formation of such a monster event. Such that we need to examine to what extent how can we better prepare for such events in the future. It is not possible to prepare for such events because it is inevitable that these storms will occur every fall and winter.

So, the notion that our planet is causing this kind of weather points to a heating atmosphere that is showing no signs of stabilizing. So far in 2019, BC has had a mild nice fall, but it has been wetter than normal and is a matter of time until those nasty storms start coming in. Once they start, it will be very hard to stop them because with every event causes those nasty wind and rain. Such that power outages and even more intense winds are forecast so time to head for the basement to ride it out.

It is the notion that in 2018 BC had a monster storm on December 20th that caused a system of sustained winds of over 100kmh in some locations leading to power outages for days, some places took at week before power was restored like the gulf islands which is an isolated area that crews cannot get to easily because it is way out of the bundle. Such that this storm was preluded by minor rain events that were annoying but didn't cause any wind. In fact, the December 20th, 2018 event was the first nasty windstorm of the season, up till that period it was nice and sunny, with some rain at times but pleasant.

Fall in BC is always mild for the first half but come mid-October is when the pattern turns to stormy and wet. The cause of concern is how much rain will fall in the autumn season because let's face it, it is a lot. For us to fully understand what is happening, it takes courage to know that our planet is letting it loose everywhere. The scary notion that every cold season in Canada especially near the coast will be victim to these nasty storms and that points a picture to climate change. If these storms don't stop, then it is evident that every year will be the same, for 4 months which is scary to think about because it is the nature of these events that raises the red flag.

The weather has always been bad in the fall-winter in BC which is typical because it is normal to have lots of rain between October-March as this is the wet season for BC. Such that each year the creek jumps its banks causing no one to be able to walk in that area which is common and windstorms causing damage and power outages, it seems normal right? However, the once normal events that only featured one nasty violent windstorm in the fall-winter is now causing multiple storms. What is so dramatic is even in the spring like April, BC is experiencing these storms, for example in 2019, BC had some bad storms in the first 1/3 of April.

Such events this late in the season point to climate change and global warming which is getting worse by the year, 2019 will not topple 2016 for the warmest year because the weak El Nino faded away, but keep in mind that 2016 record for hottest year will be broken very soon. Even these nasty rain and windstorms have occurred in late summer. For example, in 2015 at the end of August, BC had a monster windstorm that was preluded by a rainstorm. It rained the night before, then the rain stopped, and it got nice and sunny even reaching 20.c that day. However, the wind was dreadful 90km for the whole day causing the power to go out. I remember having to cancel the farmers market that Saturday because the wind was so bad.

I remember walking down to the market and seeing tents toppled and everything flying around off tables, it was horrid. This was at the end of summer which is rare for BC to have such a storm at that time of the year. However, in 2015 it happened which is the earliest storm recorded of the season and was the nastiest august storm on record for BC. Those that were in the cowichan valley then remember how bad it was because it was preluded by a very hot summer. The reality is that the rest of the fall-winter season didn't feature any storms of that caliber.

If we can have these storms in august, then these storms can occur in hot summer months causing lots of damage and this is the cause of concern because it seems that all the efforts to prepare for such events raises the question that there is nothing we can do, the world is at risk of losing forests due to these high wind events, and the rain causing damage to properties and vice versa. Such that if the world is this angry now, how bad will it be in 50 years, hurricane like storms in the fall for BC toppled 120km with every passing event.

In fact BC has had some hurricane force wind events in the colder half of the year which is a cause for concern, BC has even had the remnants of tropical storms that wreaked havoc on the pacific but weakened while they headed east towards the island. However, the effects were bad in that the wind and rain was terrible in certain places of the coast of BC. Such that there were warnings and watches for these storms as far as I can remember every single storm raised anxiety that it would be very bad.

I personally hate windstorms because they freak me out with the gusts and seeing the trees sway the feeling like they are about the snap and hit the window breaking it. Usually when I see the wind this storm, I go crazy because I know that we have had hurricane force winds in the cowichan valley and with each event raises the risk of being caught in the storm. However, I am dare taker meaning I go out in these events to test the wind speeds because knowing that if I start to rise in the sky, I realize that my weight is being shifted by the wind, it is like it is pushing me. I enjoy these storms when the winds are at the peak because it is mother nature at her worst and trust me, she is wicked when provoked.

Every fall I know that these storms will happen because it is natural for the storm track to head towards Vancouver Island and the mainland BC. However, the interior and north BC is sparred because the Jetstream divers the track away from those locations which stay dry. It is the force of nature in the fall and winter that make it interesting for people who are storm chasers to view the incredible wind and rain. BC is like a stormy fungus in the fall and winter because of the Jetstream and this will continue even in years where fall seems to be summer-like. Eventually that summer pattern will break apart if at the end of October, the last day hitting 20.c till spring of next year. The reality is that the nice fall weather will be replaced by wet weather as this is natural as we head towards the winter months.

Even in dry fall years, the storm track is similar in late fall and winter because of the change in wind patterns and speeds. Such that every single time we think that fall will not turn bad because it is hitting 20.c every day in October, think again come November it could be in the single digits as daytime highs and very wet. It is such to ponder the reality that BC is in the bullseye of any stuff that comes from the Pacific Ocean because it is nearest to it. Thus, it is stated that our planet will not tolerate us to pollute it and deforest it without serious consequences. These effects are already being felt in many areas of the world not used to seeing such extreme weather events.

Therefore, in such events it is to ponder how did the world get to this state? It wasn't like this 35 years ago in the 1980s, in fact it has never been this bad for storms and other events in the fall-winter seasons. However, it must be noted that our best efforts to understand that our planet will explode is causing a global catastrophe, and the reality of a fallen system that humans are to blame for everything mother nature feels is clear.

BC and the rest of the world need to realize that wind and rainstorms are the new norm of climate change thus causing lots of damage because of our society that continues to waste resources and pollute the planet. It is no wonder why our oceans are becoming the focal point of more extreme systems, it is evident that this world is heating up rapidly and this is causing a bad event waiting to happen. What will it take for people to realize that BC and rest of the world suffering through these nasty wind and rainstorms are the target of a stormy world that will only get stormier in coming decades?

How long until the world wakes up and sees the damage caused by these wind and rainstorms and think holy cow this is awful. It is only then that people will change and view the threat of future storms and chaos the new norm, it is the reality of a world that needs to understand that these storms are being fueled by the Jetstream and the cycle of weather that happens in the fall-winter which is scary to consider knowing what it will take to change the ways that we tend to go.

Getting back to rain and windstorms in BC trust me they are freaky to watch and experience because the thought of having to plan for power outages and days missed from work and school seems evident that our planet is warning us of danger ahead, yet we don't pay any attention to the signs all around us and don't think about what the future will look like if there are less trees due to the forests being ripped because of these storms.

That means less creatures like birds in the trees because their habitat is destroyed but the fierce windstorms and the branches snapped causing in the spring the leaves to not come back on the trees because there is so much damage from windstorms of the last fall season. There are trees in duncan BC that will never come back to life because they were uprooted from the intense windstorms and thus are winter-like year-round. These trees will have to be cut down because they aren't alive anymore which seems like it is a reality check that the amount of money costs to cut down a tree is high.

Think about the reality of seeing less trees, means less shade in the summer when it gets hot and less greenery which makes it seem natural to view the valley. However, as noted it doesn't matter to most people because they don't think this is the reality, but it is. Plus, homes that have to be remodeled because of damage from windstorms that would cost so much money and it is not funny, it is reality and the truth.

The cost of materials to remodel these homes and the work that will be needed to be done from carpenters is outrageous. This is happening every year because of these storms and it seems evident to me that people only pay attention to a nasty event but after it passes think okay that won't happen again. This is called poor thinking because these storms are happening every fall-winter, it is no longer calm and nice, it is stormy and anxious because knowing there is no escape from the effects of mother nature releasing her wrath on this world. She doesn't show mercy because she is vey upset and we are to blame for her temper.

Fishing has been scarce in BC due to these storms polluting the waters with trees and other stuff that kills the fish. I enjoy fishing myself and not seeing any salmon in the river and lakes points to the reality that our world is becoming depopulated of these small species that is having a ripple effect for marine life and anything that goes with it. Such that with every stormy event and rainstorm causing the water to flood, the water needed for fish to survive is becoming less of a reality and more of something to seek out. Personally, there are less fish because of the systems becoming more intense and the water being a source that fish don't want to go into because it will make them sick.

With less fish in the bodies of water, it seems evident to ask what now? The answer only seems evident to answer with it is warmer water that is making the habitat of fish less noticeable. To think about this and ponder how bad it is, just look at the river the next time you try to go fishing and catch nothing, the reality is there are NO fish.

If there were fish, the net would be filled with salmon to cook and eat, but you have to go to the ocean to find fish as the small bodies of water don't harbor them because of nasty storms causing their habitat to shrink and become chaotic meaning they cannot survive in such conditions. I remember when one was able to fish in the cowichan river and caught lots of salmon but that was before 2000 like in the 70s and 80s. The natives used to catch fish all the time in prime conditions and this was the say that the planet was calmer back then, however now it is a screaming lion.

The final thought is to reflect on what these storms do to the reality of a planet that only wants us to steward it, but we don't listen. Every year that we get these storms, it causes us distress seeing mother nature at her worst, yet how do we respond? We shrug it off as it is not that bad, but look around the world at these events and think about this "Do we want our future generations to experience this 3* worse? That question needs to be ground in us, before change is channeled to stop mother nature from exploding in rage.

CHAPTER 7

The next reality is the Jetstream which is becoming more erratic with each passing year. As a result of climate change our weather is not as stable as it once was. We have snow in the summer in parts of Canada for example in July 2019, Alberta and part of the BC interior had snow which isn't common for this time of the year. It is usually above 30.c in July for the BC interior but this year in 2019 it was anything but summer.

The usual desert like conditions went into winter mode and this is due to climate change and the Jetstream that is stagnant. The Jetstream is defined by how the weather travels from place to place and it is different each day in every location. Some places it snows, some it rains, some it is sunny, some is cloudy, and some are thunderstorms. It is what the Jetstream does that determines what our seasonal outlooks shape up to be. If the Jetstream favors a certain pattern, then the weather will follow.

In 2019, BC has had an unstable Jetstream similar to recent years, but this time was crazy starting in January where it was your typical wet pattern. This was followed in February by cold and snowy like coldest on record, then came March which started cool and dry and went to summer-like and record breaking. April followed and was wet for 1st half, then very dry for rest of month. May and June were very dry and hot, then came July, which was wet and mild, August was mild and dry, then September very wet and October turning dry again.

It is evident that BC and Canada have been the direct impact of a Jetstream that features a pattern of blocking of the weather to the point it doesn't change for quite some time. In fact, it stays the same for months which is what BC had in 2019 with the drought, it was the worst ever recorded as previously stated in recent chapter. However, what is a concern is that every year is the same meaning there is no change. Such a reality points to the bigger picture of the climate change theory which states that they Jetstream is favored to continue to be erratic until the world is crazy weather all over.

In part of the world there have been snowstorms in places that don't get such events, and sandstorms which aren't common but are due to the Jetstream being the way it is. Usually the Jetstream changes because of climate patterns that prevent the stream to be locked for a certain amount of time, however it is not always the case in the reality of the world becoming more freakish and temperament. These events cause the reality of a planet that is weird in weather and thus it always is #1 in headlines every week with the weather being the most talked about factor on the agenda, next being the economy.

It is the erratic weather caused by Jetstream shifts that point to the reality that our world is becoming a hot zone for activity of extreme weather that isn't normal, some places could be 10.c above normal while others are 5.c below normal. The normality of it isn't sticking to the prospects of having a climate that features this type of Jetstream that isn't stable which is not very exciting to view if you consider the weather is #1 think people talk about.

People didn't used to talk about the weather at one point because it was normal variations of ups and down. However, now people are viewing the weather as something that is out of sync and thus is causing most to rethink the reality of the Jetstream being the main factor in our weather that seems to be drifting from one extreme to the next. Such stagnant patterns are frustrating for farmers and others who rely on stable weather patterns to direct their activities and thus is very fasciation to examine how out weather influences how people view their experience.

People always check the weather before venturing out knowing what the conditions will be, it could change from day to day because of the Jetstream and how it operates, and this is very concerning that the once I didn't care what it was outside attitude now is shifted to examining that something is off. Even experts are saying it is abnormal because the weather patterns are not the way they were before, and this is the cause of numerous studies that point to the bigger picture of man-made fossil fuels and climate change.

If the Jetstream is the way it is right now, how more extreme can it get, to the point it is 6.c in July in BC and 22. C in January in BC. I mean that would be striking because that isn't normal for that region at that time of the year. However, with the Jetstream anything is possible and thus is a cause for reflection on what is causing the stream to become the way it is, it is us that is causing it with our activities that only hinder what mother nature views as adequate.

Thus, the next topic is rising sea levels which point to the reality of climate change and thus the experts have warned us for years that due to global warming, oceans will rise. Such events will be notated in many parts of the world where the sea levels are threatening nearby cities and countries. However, what is to be noted is that the warmer water is creating ripe conditions for the sea levels to keep rising, thus is the result of the warmer world that promotes such more water that has nowhere to go but on land.

People think that rising sea levels only happen on the coast of the countries that border the ocean, that is true, but it happens everywhere that harbors a body of water. It is to examine the effects of rising sea levels on the world at large from damage to homes, and hazardous materials that come from sea onto land. However, most of the effects are not pinned to the rising sea levels, but to what is in the water because there is so much garbage thrown into the ocean by humans, companies that waste their materials and even animals that poop in the water.

Rising sea levels are caused by melting glaciers meaning the normal ice isn't as consistent as once thought because the water is too warm to sustain the ice needed to keep the water cold. In arctic, the ice is melting away like crazy and soon it will be all gone meaning nothing up north. Therefore, the sea level will rise because the ice isn't keeping it solid and the water is evaporating from the ice cube to increase the water flow in the oceans. Once that water heats up with the sun, it becomes warmer and expands.

If the sea levels rise everywhere across the globe considering that majority of earth is water, then it is evident that the rising sea levels will lead to land areas becoming rivers and lakes. This seems evident already in places of the world that used to be land, but because of rising sea levels, it has turned into a body of water. If these small locations are being wiped out by rising sea levels, then what does it state for the rest of the world that is protected by huge areas of land. It states that the climate is the driving force behind the rising sea levels which will threaten anything that comes in the way of reducing the load.

Therefore, action must be taken to prevent such effects from occurring because it is becoming bad enough that these small areas that were once harbored by land are being washed away by the rising sea levels. The warmer planet is to blame for everything that the water does because it has nowhere to go but onto the land of the nearest location wiping it out slowly taking a lot of time but still it is enough to ponder why it is happening so soon.

Sooner or later, this world will be in jeopardy if sea levels keep rising, salmon a risk, other species at risk and human health at risk especially in parts of the world that are poor in general and don't have access to clean resources like the western world has access to. If rising sea levels don't get your hair spiked, then what will the destruction of cities due to rising levels of water. This is why we need to adjust our living and change our ways to prevent these events from occurring, it is only common sense to do something to preserve what we have left because it is going away like crazy and won't come back.

Those places where the sea level has wiped out will never return to their location because there is nothing there anymore but water. Soon this whole world will be water and no land, if this is scary enough to shake your head over, then you know what to do, change your ways. Humans aren't ready to adapt to the rising sea levels because it doesn't seem evident that it could happen in place like North America, but it already is. Such a reality is the notion that if we don't think about these effects before, they occur, then what does that say about us? It states that we desire to lead a life that is laid back and thinking oh the news comes on; it isn't happening here so not to worry. What if I happened on the west coast of BC, then what would people do?

The problem is people don't think about how rising sea levels could impact them because they don't think it can affect anything that matters. The wrong thinking here is to assume it never will happen and thus the planet will spare their location. If mother nature spared a location from her wrath, then it is evident she cares for parts of the world, but newsflash she doesn't care who she strikes with her fury because let's face it, everyone is a target for rising sea levels. It is not just the coasts of the countries; it is everywhere across the globe because water is the most common element in this world. Final thought is to reflect on what the future will be if the sea levels rise to the point there is no going back, it is scary to ponder this as most would become aware of the reality of a world that is only going to get wetter. The more rain, the more water and the more water, the worse of it will be, time to think about this.

CHAPTER 8

The focus now is on the past warm periods of the globe because let's face it this current spike in temperatures in the modern era is the most extreme than ever before. It states that global warming is worse right now than it was 500 years ago, and this is a major issue that needs to be addressed because the past warm periods weren't man-made climate change, it was natural cycles of warming of the globe. Such that if we look at how hot it has been since the late 1800s, it is evident that climate change is in a warm phase now meaning global temperatures are rising each year, the question now is will it keep in the warm phase for another 300 years, or another nasty ice age will follow, stay tuned.

To question the last warm period was nicknamed "medieval warm period" which saw the temperatures increase around the world and this lasted from 900-1300 thus 400-year event that was consistent with historical records showing that this was indeed a very warm period globally. The effects of such an event are portrayed in the reality that it was hot back in those times but not as hot as the current spike. Let's think back to what the weather was like in those 400 warm years, it was impressive as it was consistent.

The causes of this warm period according to the historical data show increased solar activity meaning the sun was higher at the previous point that it was after that period ended. With the increased solar activity, it results in the sun being expanded at a higher rate, therefore the sun is stronger than it would be if the solar activity was lower. Thus, the temperature increased during this period because the earth got hotter with increase solar activity from the sun.

Another cause of this warm period was a reduction in volcanic activity which makes sense knowing that when volcanoes happen, the lava is shooed into the air cooling the planet. This creates a barrier that the sun cannot get through as well as it could if the volcanic activity weren't happening. The theory that the lava is released causing the air to become cooler is the theory as to why the little ice age followed this warm period and that is the next chapter but for now is the warm periods. Such an event of low volcanic activity points to the reality of a climate that was non active in terms of eruptions of lava from mountains.

The third cause is a change in ocean circulation meaning the waters weren't as cold as usual and became much warmer for some reason that we don't know for sure quite yet. It is possible the lack of ice in that period contributed to the oceans becoming less circulated with the cool waters needed to prevent it from becoming hotter in terms of sea levels. However, as the past indicates, the causes of such a warm event due to ocean circulation are as biased as we know for a certain fact what is causing the current warm period that is worse than the 900-1300 period.

The effects of such a warm period have been documented worldwide as a study that portrays how warm it was. To question that this current spike in temperature over this period is the evidence that global warming has been going on for a long time and the effects have been pronounced for such that time frame.

The effects are the reality of winters that were drier and warmer than normal in North America and the world at large. Thus, there wasn't any snow or cool temperatures in the winter and therefore it was not white and cold like usual. The milder winters had a major impact such that without that moisture in the form of snow, many winter activities back in those days were non-existent because it didn't get cold due to the warmer winters that occurred every year. Such effects are consistent with the theory that this was a very warm period that the world experienced due to the natural climate change effect.

Thus, the growing seasons were longer, and it was hotter in the spring-fall especially summers that were very hot and dry. Drought was a big problem in this period due to lack of rain and warm temperatures that prevented any precipitation from reaching the surface. North America experienced major droughts every summer and even lack of rain meant crops had to be harvested early or did not survive because it was so hot and dry.

The model of how warm it was points to the reality that climate change was evident back in those 400 years and the effects of it with droughts, fires and heatwaves signal the notion that global warming was there in those days. However, with this period wasn't caused by man-made pollution of greenhouse gases and other things like deforestation, it was caused by the natural effects of circulation as well as other factors that have not contributed to the current global warming spike.

The next historical warm period was the "Roman Warm Period" which lasted between 250-400 meaning it was only 150 years but still had major global impacts in temperature and precipitation levels. This mostly effected Europe and the Northern Atlantic thus being the less nasty than the medieval period but still a cause for discussion and reflection. During this period, it was the same as the most recent one prior to the current global warming cycle which will be talked about later in this chapter. However, during the roman warm period, it was noted that the temperatures were very warm during the winter for Europe and North Atlantic as well as worldwide, but Europe suffered the brunt of the heat.

Such a warm period is the result of global warming and its natural cycle of being warm and cool thus alternating between the two and this was a typical warm period that resulted in increased temperatures on land in the globe. However, it wasn't as warm as the 900-1300 event nor as warm as the current event. This is the talk of discussion because if we look at this period of warmth, it is hardly evident it was hotter than this. Our climate has gotten warmer since this event and the other 400 year one just talked about, it is the reality of such weaker warm events that point to climate change that wasn't forced on by humans, that was natural due to the effects of normal circulation and patterns like volcanic activity. Therefore, it is safe to assume that the previous two warm events prior to the current point the picture that this is the worst it's been.

The reality that the earth has experience past warm periods that have lasted between 150-400 years which means that the globe has warmed. However, the current warm period is the worst it has ever been, it basically points to a pattern that has never been seen before and thus a cause for ponder and worry. The future is guarded because it seems this warm period is only getting worse, while the historical ones didn't get worse, they remained the same throughout the years present. However, it must be stated that the world is warmer today than it was 1000 years ago, and this is a cause to reflect on this current warm phase being nastier than any warm events of the past.

The difference between this current event and past ones is that those before the little ice age weren't caused by humans, they were caused by natural cycles of the earth. The current event began in 1850 or around that period continuing since so over 150 years into it and getting more hotter as we go along. It wasn't that bad in the early 20th century as it wasn't as hot as it is now in the 21st century. However, the effects started getting worse by the 1980s. In the 1970s there was a mini cool down worldwide during that decade and temperatures weren't as warm as the previous six decades but still a cause for ponder that global warming has intensified in the last 40 years.

These last 40 years from 1980-2019 were the hottest on record in history and this is continuing to strengthen as each passing year will be hotter than the year before. In fact, the 2010s are warmer than the 2000s. The 2000s are warmer than the 1990s, and the 1990s are warmer than the 1980s. Each decade is warmer than the last and this wasn't the case with the last warm periods in history because as stated, it wasn't man-made, it was natural.

However, it must be noted that the current model suggests that the 2020s will be warmer than the 2010s and each decade will be warmer than the last. The picture come 2100 is a climate that is too hot to sustain any form of life and this suggest that global warming is not going away this time. Usually with past events, it was followed by a nasty ice age to cool the planet again, but this time the ice age wont happen, it will just get hotter till we are in a robotic age that will only feature robots as he only life source.

Such a scary picture of the future of this planet when in doubt it seems that with past warm periods, there was a natural cause behind the warmth, now as science has evolved and humans have electricity and other things not observed back in those days, it is evident that humans are more capable of destroying this planet and causing the warmth to become intense. However, back in those days of past warm periods, we didn't have electricity or vehicles running on gas, or internet or phones or things to pollute the air. It didn't exist because it hadn't been made yet, those people relied on other methods to survived which was good for the planet due to the reality of lack of resources, the earth couldn't be polluted with greenhouse gases.

As a result of not having such things back in those days was evident in the way those folk lived, they cherished the planet because technology was non existent back them, they didn't have clocks to tell time even, so one had to view the sun to determine what time of the day it was. Thus, if the current humanity of resources is lacking due to the notion that our day and age has everything and thus is increasing. Digital technology didn't exist even 30 years ago but now it does.

Getting back to the current model of temperature spike this world is experiencing, it must be noted that it is only a matter of time until this world is shriving to destroy what mother nature created. The cause of this current global warming is humans, not natural cycles of the ocean circulation or anything else that would be the driver for past warm periods, so it is to examine how then are humans going to adapt to a future that wont favor any relief.

Since 1998 which was the warmest year on record due to a strong El Nino which being the strongest on record for that time, since we have broken numerous records 2005, 2010, 2014, 2015 and 2016 were the warmest years. In fact, the last 15 years have featured the 2000-2019 period being the warmest. The last decade saw 7/10 of the last top 10 warmest years on record due to man-made global warming. 2016 is the current hottest year on record but 2019 is creeping up to either get 2nd place or tie for warmest on record. It is a matter of time until 2016 is broken as that year was very warm due to the strongest El Nino ever.

The weather patterns with this current warm period are evident and occurring every year with droughts, fires, heatwaves and other depletion of salmon and lack of water. BC has experienced every single year drought since 2010 minus 2011 and 2012 which were La Nina years. However, the current rate of global warming isn't just affecting temperature, it is the cause of many species becoming extinct due to it being too hot to sustain the life. With the rivers drying out and the oceans becoming populated with all these chemicals, it is evident it will only get hotter in the summer. It is reaching 50.c in some parts of the globe during the summer which didn't happen during the previous warm periods.

If the models are correct, then this planet will look like a desert all over in 50 years due to the increase in temperatures and thus man-made global warming isn't stopping, in fact it will continue until humans self-destruct this planet and cause the warming to sustain and worsen. The experience of it being so hot is evident in the growing seasons that are extended every year, and water restrictions in October. This is due to global warming and the increased high pressure that is sustained causing the temperature to hit 20.C in late October in part of the western half of Canada. Normally when it should be cooling down, some years have been in the low 20s in October for like a week before the Jetstream changes causing the cooler air to circulate, but that isn't happening like it did.

The worry now is how hotter will it get with this current warm period? How high can the temperature get to? The reality is that it will not stop increasing in temperature if man-made global warming continues, if deforestation continues, as long as pollution of the air continues and seas. This is the notion that our world is falling apart because people only care for themselves than for a planet that is overheating worse than ever before. In the past, there was always something that would stop the warm period putting an end to it, but this time around there might not be any hope that a cooling will occur.

The hope of a cooldown seems evident but will never happen because man-made global warming is the driver these days to fuel the businesses that rely on this to expand. However, it must be stated that if global warming gets any worse, it will indeed lead to a future that it will be 20.C in BC every year from even November-February. This hasn't happened yet as it has never reached 20.C between November 1st and February 28th. During this period in BC along the coast it is below 10.c most days but with climate change, we could get heatwaves in the winter season leading to those records of only hitting 17.C as a max extreme high for November being broken.

It is not just BC and western Canada, it is everywhere that the temperature is hotter even in cool places like Iceland are hotter than they have ever been due to climate change and the current warm period as stated will not stop until is too hot for anything to thrive. The question is how do we change our ways to reverse this process restoring the planet to what it was just after the last ice age or is it too late? It might already be too late to do anything now as we may have already warmed this planet changing to current patterns to an extent that any actions to reduce climate change are not likely going to have any affect.

If the reality of a warmer world is scary, think about what it took for it to become this hot? It was hot before, we did have recent warm periods prior to the little ice age which will be talked about in the next chapter a break from all the warming. However, it is a story worth discovering why our planet keeps warming and what if anything can be done to prevent and stabilize this planets core temperature.

Scientists think an asteroid or nuclear winter might help, but these things are rare meaning never to happen, so if we have many volcanic eruptions like we did causing the last ice age, can it happen again? The answer lies in the reality of how warm will the planet get until it reached the peak, then it will have to cool down right? Think of the peak the middle point thus being the climax, after something reaches the peak, it slowly goes down. Take IQ tests, the mean score is 100, so I slowly decline until you reach 160. Therefore, there will be a peak in year period where global warming is at its worst, the question is when will that happen?

Thus, the final point is to realize that this is the hottest its ever been and probably will be. There will be an end to this current warm period, the question is what will it take to achieve this effect? Will it be the extinction of humanity to achieve it? The answer lies in understand what it will take for the planet to finally cool down leading to an ice age that will restore that temperature putting an end to global warming but for now climate change is domination, time to adjust to the yearly effects.

CHAPTER 9

The next topic is the little ice age which followed the last warm period being the reality that one day global warming or the current warm period will turn cold. However, the reality of this happening anytime soon is no likely because global warming is so pronounced, it will take lots of time until the planet changes course and it starts to cool down. This is likely the result of discussion that we must adapt to talk about if the planet is to stabilize which in turn would reverse global warming thus ending all the pain and destruction of the current heatwaves that are impacting the globe at large.

To understand the little ice age is to comprehend how it happened because the earth had a warm period before it took shape, but the reality of the ice age following such a warm period seems evident that our planet does go up and down in terms of temperature and trends. What is fascinating then is to realize that our planet is on guard and eventually will cool off, it always does in the fall in the Northern Hemisphere staying that way till the spring, hence the cool half of the year. What seems evident then is to assume all will continue even in years that we have very hot summers because that is natural of the sun becoming less high in the sky. During the month of October, the sun isn't as high as it would be in April, therefore the air starts to cool down and this is normal, but the little ice age wasn't normal as it was a extended period of cool weather across the globe.

The little ice age was an extended period of cold weather across the global starting right after the last warm period ended around 1300 lasting till 1850. This is 550 years of cool weather that showed no mercy across parts of the globe, which is scary considering the warm period only lasted 400 years. So, 150 more years for the little ice age states that there was a very great cool down after that medieval warm period which by history was very warm.

The effects of such an ice age were evident across the global with the most severe of the snap occurring during the maunder minimum which occurred between 1645 to 1715, thus being the worst part of the ice age where it was at its worst. Thus, if the evidence of such a cold period makes one shake, it is evident that our planet was very quiet and cold back then meaning lots of cold winters and short summers.

The causes of such an ice age are documented in the reality of the reverse of what caused the previous warm period that happened before the start of such an ice age. One of the causes was low solar activity and this was very bad during the Maunder Minimum which occurred between 1645 and 1715, this was the worst part of the cold age because the sun was its at lowest during those years, one can imagine how cold it was during that period.

Think of the Maunder Minimum as a scary thought of a pattern only consistent with winter but instead of it lasting 3 months, it lasts half a year to a year in some locations. To think that Mexico can be cold year-round is ridiculous because it is always hot, but in the case of the ice age not so much which is scary to point the blame on the one thing. However, it is the notion of a reduced solar flow that was to blame for the cool down that resulted in severe cold winters globally during that period.

Volcanic activity was another factor being the more lava introduced into the air, the more it prevents the sun from shining through and thus creates a cooldown. Since the planet needs the sun to warm the earth, if the sun is blocked out by the lava accumulating into the air, it cannot warm up, so the sun doesn't shine as well causing the clouds to prevent a warmup.

Whenever we have volcanoes you know it will not be as hot because of the lava spewed from such events which in turn causes the sun to become weaker thus resulting in the clouds becoming darker and thus the air becoming cooler as a result. The scary notion that our globe has experience volcanic eruptions points to nature, but during the ice age, there was lots of volcanic eruptions that caused the planet to undergo what was a massive shift in climatic patterns which is scary to think about but the truth is out there.

Ocean circulation was weaker which caused the little ice age, whereas during the warm period it was stronger. However, if we were to just focus on the circulation, it has to be noted that isn't the main factor, it is more that the colder water was more significant than the warmer water that tried to accumulate the cold air but couldn't thus creating the ripe conditions for the little ice age which turned out to very bad.

The cause of alternative causes of warm periods might explain why we had such a nasty cold snap for 550 years. It is possible with the warm periods, the cold must come back to balance out the tee totter, which is normal, however for such an extreme ice age was not normal and thus a cause for concern. It must be noted then that our climate suffered a great deal during those 550 years causing what was a nasty period where the temperatures didn't rise even in the summer.

Thus, the research also states reduced human populations which don't seem to be cause of the ice age but it's kind of makes sense because humans keep the planet warm. Just the body temperature of a human being is 98.6 which is 37. C. This is hot enough to keep the cold air at bay, that is desert like heat inside each one of us. When we are sick with the flu and have a high fever, it is like we are living in Phoenix Arizona because our temperature not only keeps us warm, but the whole areas around us for some time.

The final cause is deforestation from increased human populations thus causing more cooldown. However, there were less people than there is today so what difference does it make? It makes a difference in that even with less people, deforestation can still have a major impact on the climate, even one tree cut down can damage the planet. The scary truth is that with the cut down of trees can lead to a cool down, when today it leads to increase in temperature, thus this doesn't make sense why deforestation would cause the temperature to cool? One answer could be the people deforested from high altitudes like the mountains and the research points to this.

The effects will be damaging to discuss but the ice age caused long severe winters in North America and Europe during such a period. Such coldness meant lakes froze over with ice and one could skate even on the streets it was so cold. Thus, it is possible not to even imagine how cold it was because very few people know of ancestors that were alive during that period. But the winters we had during that period were harsh and lasted a long time well into the spring, snow still falling in April.

One couldn't imagine how cold it would take to create a wintry mix that would lead to snow right up to June in some years. It is scary that the winters were so cold when the warm period previous was very warm, however as noted global cooling was at its worst during the Maunder Minimum and thus a cause for concern as noted because one cannot imagine how the species could survive such harsh cold winter conditions.

Summers were short and cool, meaning it wasn't hot and dry, it was wet and cold. Imagine a summer where it doesn't hit 20.C in BC, it is in the high teens every day with rain, this would be nasty, and one wouldn't be able to go swimming or enjoy ice cream. Now think about how it was during the last ice age, this was the reality for the whole which lived through such a period.

It is noted that the effects of this ice age were not only in North America but the globe at large, no one was immune to the cold conditions. Therefore, it is safe to assume after this ice age ended in 1850 that it wouldn't ever happen again. However, as noted in the past, the world will see another ice age in the future. It is a matter of time before the climate shifts again and trust me with global warming being as bad as it is now, in fact the current warm period is worse than the last warm period meaning the ice age that follows will be more severe than the little ice age.

Think about how cold it will be in the next ice age? Consider how cold the little ice age was? Then consider what will happen if the patterns goes worse, we are looking at 10.C below normal in the winter which would be severe and long lasting. The summer being the same drop would be dramatic meaning it wont even reach 15.C. How scary would it be for winter to occur all year long. Now realize that with global cycles of ups and downs, it is evident that the world is approaching the half-way mark of the current warm period based on how hot it is. We are approaching the peak of the current warm period, so once it ends, the ice age will follow, be ready for species that aren't extinct as a result of climate change to perish during the ice age that follows.

A final thought is to reflect on how cold it was before, to consider that the earth goes in cycles with regards to warm and cool periods, it is a matter of reality that the earth will experience another ice age, this is for certain, the question is whether we are ready for the effects of it. Study the past and determine the next course of action, don't be foolish to think the planet will not experience another ice age, it is a matter of time till global warming is no more.

CHAPTER 10

The next focus in on the period 2070-2100 because this is when the worst of global warming will occur because of the greenhouse effect. It is already very hot right now due to climate change and the question is how hotter can it get? The reality is the temperature will keep rising each decade till we reach an environment that will not be able to sustain any life and the next chapter focuses on the species that are already becoming extinct due to climate change, so by 2100, there might not be any species in animals due to climate change.

The reality is this period is most alarming because of how hot it will be and the effects that will be felt across the globe. However, it must be noted that if the science is right, then the planet will not be able to cool itself in the winter thus being summer-like all year-long. This sounds scary but is the truth and thus is a cause for reflection on what needs to be done to combat climate change before it gets this bad.

Reality is that there is nothing we can do now because the damage may already have been done to the world due to global warming, it is safe to bet it will only become worse. However, government officials are trying to combat climate change by hosting various climate strikes which wake up the public of the effects of climate change. The severity of the planet warming is evident even today with all the heatwaves and droughts plus forest fires becoming more severe and frequent.

One might think it is hot now and this is no joke, it is very abnormal in terms of heat, but come 2050 heading all the way till 2100, there are maps showing hot hotter it will be. Thus, the experts are saying it will be 5.C warmer in places such as BC every month meaning BC will not get any winters. The scary reality is how hot can it get in BC being will it hit 20.C in January and heatwaves every month of the year. The effects of climate change make it possible to examine the notion that extreme weather events will become nastier during this last half of the century. There is evidence to suggest it will get bad in BC but everywhere that is cold right now, the arctic ice will no longer exist due to climate change.

The 1st effect is the warmer temperatures in BC, 5. C warmer than average will look like Victoria being 11. C in January 13. C in February, 15. C in March, 18. C in April, 21. C in May, 24. C in June, 27. C in both July and August, 24. C in September, 19. C in October, 14. C in November and 12. C in December. These are the normal high temperatures for each month or what it will be in Victoria BC, that is near the water, other inlands places like Nanaimo or even the interior of BC will be much hotter. Therefore, the extreme high temperatures being the highest it can go in the month will become 5. C warmer than they currently are.

I couldn't even imagine how hot it could get in winter months, it could hit 21.C and close to 40.C in the summer being the most extreme connection that we have ever seen. However, this is being studied and scientists have concluded the models they have, this is a real 100% possibility and it is no joke.

With winter heatwaves, there would be no snow on the mountains, ski resorts would have to shut down because it is too mild to even snowboard. The reality of any Olympic games that will be held would have to be cancelled due to the winters being summer-like which is a definite reality that BC would have to adapt to. This is the notion that our part of the world isn't immune to the effects of climate change, BC has had very mild winters already without any snow, so it's a matter of time until every year is hot enough to go swimming in the lake. Can one imagine swimming in the river in January? It could be hot enough come 2080 to do such a thing because of the 20.C spike BC will experience due to climate change.

Thus, we have to adapt to this now as our summers are becoming hotter, and our winters warmer being the reality in 2019 going on 2020, it is only a matter of time until BC is as warm as the California state and even Arizona in the interior. Places like any desert right now that hits 40.C in summer months come 2070 will not be able to sustain any life, it will be too hot and those people would have to flock to cooler areas, but good luck finding any area that will be out of the woods, everywhere will be hotter, even Iceland will be hitting the high teens. Although this would be enough of a relief, but the population of that country would be overwhelmed with millions of people escaping super-hot conditions.

The 2nd effect is increased rainfall in the winter months for BC due to climate change. It has to be noted that the rainstorms in fall-winter in BC are bad right now, but can one only imagine in 2070-2080 how nasty the rainstorms will be, it could be torrential rain and hurricane force winds not only once a season but every month 4 times at least maybe 6. The storms will become so intense that BC will experience category 1 hurricanes with wind gusts of 119-153 kph during the winter months when usually it is cold enough in the waters to prevent such nasty storms. Climate change will lead to more flooding along the coast causing state of emergencies. BC will bear the brunt of these storms because it is closer to the epicenter of these wicked warm waters.

Therefore, more damage and more power outages and definite for areas along the BC coast and other worldwide coasts. The strength of these storms could last days not just 12 hours. The duration of the rain and wind could be enough to topple trees and cause destruction in their wake. The scary reality is that every year could be this bad, come fall and winter, the weather will be stormy high winds and nasty rainstorms. However, it must be noted that BC has had winters that haven't been as bad with storms, that is not to say every winter will be nasty, some will be nastier in El Nino years than Neutral events.

The 3rd effect is major droughts in the summer due to drier conditions along the coast of BC. Right now, BC is experiencing yearly droughts in the summer with water restrictions, due to climate change. The last 3 years have been very bad between April-August meaning during that spring-summer period, BC has had extended dry spells that have dried up the grass browning it and leading to stage 4 drought conditions in 2019 never seen before. For the 1st time ever, BC coast has had to pump water out of a weir to supply the Cowichan River because it was so low due to a very dry winter and spring plus a dry summer.

It seems every year BC experiences these droughts due to climate change and the concern is that by 2070-2080, it will be very bad, BC might run out of water in the summer and thus the rivers wouldn't have any water in them, if you drive across the bridge and look down at the river and see no water, that is scary. It is scary to think BC could become like Arizona a desert-like environment that would always be dry without any water, the grass would die and become rocks like Arizona, the trees would die because of lack of moisture, therefore new trees would be planted that could sustain such dry conditions.

It will be a bad time for farmers that need water to fertilize their crops, without it, most produce wouldn't be able to thrive. The cost of food prices would be so high, people wouldn't want to even buy any groceries and most would starve because there isn't any produce on the market, think about Arizona and how hard it is to plant anything due to the drought, this could happen in BC and cause famine even in this neck of the woods. Other areas of the world that are already in famine right now will cease to exist because of drought.

The 4th effect is forest fires becoming more severe and hectic. Right now, BC has been ravaged by nasty forest fires every summer and this is becoming more severe because of global warming. Can one imagine how bad it will be in 2070-2080 due to climate change, BC could have forest fires as early as January due to climate change. Forest fires cost the province of BC millions of dollars in damage every year due to burned hectares of trees and the damage the fires cause to nearby homes and communities, it is staggering how much cost the taxpayer would have to endure because of all these fires.

The air quality is not great in the summer due to the smoke from these burning fires in BC, such years have been so bad, the sky is hot and light a wall of cloud that isn't cloud, it is smoke and prevents the sun from coming out. There have been years that BC has had the air quality so bad with fires, people with allergies would have to stay inside or wear a mask just to prevent symptoms. It seems that it will become the reality that the air would become so polluted, people wouldn't be able to walk down the street due to smoke burning from wildfires. It seems scary to think this could happen, but this is how bad it could get by 2070-2080 due to wildfires that are burning out of control or keep burning for weeks on end. The smoke filling the sky wouldn't be for 1 week, it could be for the whole summer if the fires are burning.

The 5th effect is increase in allergies and respiratory conditions that would be more people sick and suffer longer. Allergy season is already extended due to climate change starting early in the spring and lasting till the late fall. Allergies by 2070-2080 could be year-long bad all year long. The winters and warmer climate would make for some very bad allergy years causing great misery and suffering among more people.

To have allergies is like having a cold that never ends, usually bad colds end in 10-14 days, but allergies can last for months. With climate change becoming more severe, allergies will become more severe and longer seasons with more suffering and more sleepless nights due to congestion and coughing. The reality is that our planet is already too warm for many people, and this will become to an extent of being very hot to the point it will not matter which area of the globe you live in, you will become sick even during the winter. Thus, cold and flu season will be shorter and milder but allergy season severe and long-lasting. Flowers starting to bulb in January and trees gaining leaves in February, could be green by late February with all those flowers and insects, it will be a haven for agony. To state it wouldn't get this bad is foolish to assume that our planet can keep up protecting us from the effects of our own arrogant decisions we make every day. Other illnesses like Malaria could become widespread across the globe due to increased temperatures as well as nasty fevers that could sickness lots of people in BC.

The sickness resulted from climate change could lead to millions of dollars lost in terms of workplace absenteeism. Many people wouldn't be able to work as much due to the polluted air becoming worse and lead to not going outside as much, business that relies on customers would suffer a great deal especially in summer months and this would lead those businesses to shutdown because of lack of customers, in fact all it takes for a business to shorten their hours is a drop in people visiting the store, the less people the less likely the business will stay open and thus closing earlier than usual.

The 6th effect is summer sports and activities that wont be able to happen because it being too hot, with lack of water due to drought and hot enough to not want to go outside, most of the activities such as camping, hiking and even going on the water will not happen because many people don't want to get heatstroke. Just going outside would prove a challenge because with it being so hot, many people would only go out at night or early in the morning. Thus, if the heat prevents people from venturing outside, that is a big hit for the sports industry that will most doubt take a hit downward during the hot summer months. The campgrounds being sparse, water and beaches not anyone, many pools and mountains not avid with hikers, it would be like Arizona in the summer, too hot to even do anything. Working in offices without air conditioning would become a task just to make it through the day without fainting. Once you got home from work, you would want to take a nice cold bath, the thought of any exercise between 10am and 4pm, don't count on it.

If this is the reality, then it seems plausible to assume that people wouldn't enjoy summer anymore like they used to because the focus would be on the heat. With it being 30.C every day without a break, it would become impossible to have the energy to do anything because when it gets that hot, your energy is zapped. Just being outside is not very great since your body would heat up quickly, if you sick with any illness, it feels worse to be outside even when its 20.C +. This is the scary reality that summer for most on BC island isn't as bad as the interior but the longer it stays above 30.C, the more likely of diarrhea and related illnesses.

The final effect is the reality of knowing that our weather is already becoming hotter by the year and it is extended days above 20.C that is evident. In 2019, The cowichan area had 123 days above 20.C, this is the 2nd longest streak behind 2015. Thus, if the models are correct, it could be half the year come 2070 that is above the 20.C mark. When it gets hotter, the result is increased radiation from the air and thus more people will be at risk for skin cancer. However, those nights won't be as cool meaning it might not cool down. In 2019, there were nights it didn't get below 20.C until 3am. Thus, this past summer wasn't as hot as recent ones, but the humidex was up everyday meaning it felt hotter than it was.

To summarize the effects of the period leading up to 2100, it is evident that these effects are starting to happen right now and thus will become more pronounced until this world is too hot to sustain life. The reality is now is the time for governments to act and create plans to combat the change before it gets to that reality of no going back.

CHAPTER 11

The next focus in on the species most at risk from global warming due to man-made changes in the air. People don't realize that climate change is impacting species across the world due to the habitat of such creatures not being able to adapt to the rising temperatures experienced on both land and sea. These creatures cannot adapt as well as humans can because their bodies work differently than the human being. The species take heat much more extreme than humans do because they aren't naturally inclined to feel such heat that is only getting worse. Such species need cool environments to thrive such that those species can survive.

The reality is people don't realize how bad it is and the species most at risk from human caused global warming because we don't think about our species. We think we are the only species out there that is huge in numbers cause in the billions while the other species aren't as populated. However, what must be stated is that humans must need to take care of their other species of creatures that god created. He didn't just create man and woman, he created birds, animals, mammals and other sea creatures. The reality is that these species will become extinct if climate change continues at the rapid rate it currently is. Scary thought how bad can it get before all species around the globe are extinct and thus these species provide food for us, that is where we get our meat from. So, if climate change destroys these species, it is safe to assume that people aren't caring about the other species, just themselves.

The 1st species at risk is the tiger which might seem to be irrelevant because these creatures can survive hot conditions, they are found in Africa and other desert-like climates, so why are they at risk? Who knows the answer to this question because it seems that people don't know that tigers cannot take very hot temperatures? Only to a certain degree, but anything hotter than 35.C, they will not be able to thrive. It is uncanny to think that these creatures can become extinct because they naturally thrive in hot conditions, it is stated that Africa and places like that are usually hot year-round, but the reality of it getting hotter due to climate change is putting these species at risk.

The reason behind why tigers could become extinct sounds irrelevant because these creatures are so strong and able to withstand anything. However, climate change is a feature that most species cannot withstand, humans cannot withstand hot conditions, and thus this species have lower body temperatures than humans. It is perishable that we know when climate change is worsening because it is impeccable that these species of tiger are at risk more than any other species because they are naturally from hot climates but there aren't any tigers in desert areas because it is too hot for them. The question is how bad can climate change become so these species cannot survive? It has to be noted that the hotter it gets, the more at risk these species are, and the likelihood of them becoming extinct is evident.

The 2nd species at risk of extinction are whale species which is evident since these species mostly live in water conditions. Whales aren't land creatures, if they wandered onto land, they would suffocate and cease to exist. The worry is because the droughts are continuing and getting worse, these previous creatures are having their habitat poisoned by waste from landfills as well as warmer waters that don't promote survival. These creatures need cool conditions in order to survive, if they don't get those right conditions, they won't make it.

It is interesting to note how these creatures make it through the hotter months? They must migrate to cooler waters in other parts of the world that don't get as hot. It is absurd to think that these creatures cannot thrive in such hot conditions because of their nature. However, whales need to be surrounded by water to thrive. If the rivers and oceans get too hot, these creatures will become extinct due to the warming of the waters due to climate change. These are sea creatures meaning they need cool waters to make it through. Think of a sea creature makes it onto land or into a warm pool of water, they cannot survive because it is too hot. There bodies cannot deal with the heat and still have the energy to live, therefore they perish.

The 3rd species at risk is African Elephant hint which originates in Africa a place that is usually hot. However, one might wonder why is this creature at risk? The reality is that this creature isn't strong enough to withstand very hot conditions. These are only land creatures; they cannot be around water because they won't survive in such conditions. It is crazy to consider how these creatures can survive in other parts of the world, because Africa is the only continent they exist because it is the right environment for such a species. The reality then is to examine how bad climate change can impact these creatures. If it gets too hot, then these creatures will not be able to make it. The rainy climates cannot sustain these creatures because they are naturally a hot mammal. However, as seen with the erratic patterns of climate, even the reality of this creature becoming extinct sounds low, but it can happen with the increased volatile weather the world will continue to face until everything is gone.

The 4th species at risk is Amazon meaning this part of the globe is a special spot that has been around for many centuries. However, climate change is thinking their population a great deal due to man-made global warming that is only becoming worse. If one were to look at this part of the world and think it will not face the same effects as other species, they are wrong because everywhere is at risk. The amazon becoming extinct would be major for the rest of the world because it is such a nice spot to view and walk through. I haven't been to this part of the world, but I heard there are nice species there. If the amazon which is mostly forest becomes at risk due to climate change, it is the reality of how it can get to this? It is people that need to realize sacred spots of the world like the Amazon aren't immune to effects of increased temperatures on land and sea. If we want to save this part of the world and its species, then stop putting greenhouse gases into the atmosphere because every single time you do that, it creates a nasty environment for these parts of the world to thrive.

The 5th species at risk is Arctic creatures that thrive only in icy cold conditions. Thus these mammals are mostly only in very cold climates because of their natural layers of wool. They need this wool to survive such cold climates and thus would be too hot to make it into a temperature climate. Such creatures are natural up in the northern part of the world where it never makes it above freezing due to the sun not reaching such parts of the world. Therefore, these creatures don't need any heat because any sort of warmup can put their habitat in jeopardy. The worry is due to the warming planet, arctic ice is melting meaning these species won't be able to survive because the arctic is warming up. Never has the arctic been so hot, it is due to climate change that these species are at risk of extinction. If the arctic warms up to the point of no return, these species will not be able to survive such hot conditions and will perish.

The 6th species at risk is coastal east Africa or anything that is on the part of the continent due to it being near the water. Anything that is alive in terms of mammals in that part of the globe is at risk because the species aren't naturally equipped to deal with hot conditions and too hot meaning most will not be able to survive if the temperatures get up to what scientists forecast they will by late 21st century. However, as seen these species can adapt to slight changes in temperature, but too hot and they won't be able to survive such conditions due to the reality of not being able to cool themselves down. Other species can cool themselves down with going into the water but certain beach species near the water cannot go into the water because that is not their habitat. Therefore, it has to be stated that these species will not be able to thrive under such conditions, therefore they will become extinct sooner than later.

The 7th species at risk is the coral triangle meaning anything that is in the sea. Coral triangle is anything that is at the bottom of the ocean, thus these creatures naturally have or need habitats that are free from anything that would disturb them like heat or toxins. The reality being these species are already at risk due to bottom part of the ocean becoming contaminated with other creatures and gases people leave when boats cruise down the river. Such gases would thrive to create a nasty situation for such creatures because it isn't the water that affects these creatures, it is the environment that creates the problems.

To state that these species are at risk is the reality that even species at the bottom of the sea are at risk because the effects of warming planet reach even the farthest south. The effects don't stop once they reach the surface of the water, they go down to the end even if it is 150 feet downward. The scary reality is that the warmer the waters become, the more likely these species will not be able to thrive in such conditions. It is therefore evident that humans need to think about what they put into the ocean and if it is toxic, don't dump it because there are species at risk down there.

Such that if people were to use their brains and consider the species that they are risking with their activities, then all would favor a better outcome because the sea needs these species to stay salty. If the water isn't salty, other species like fish cannot live as well as turtles and frogs. It is evident then that global warming will destroy these habitats causing these previous species to become extinct and when the corals become extinct, then all the other ocean species will follow suite. Such a mass extinction will lead to loss of major species in the world that rely on this method of saltwater that isn't salty because climate change has altered the patterns.

The 8th species at risk is dolphins because they are a water mammal. The effect of warming waters creates a prime sample of what can happen if it gets too hot for these creatures to survive. The reality is that these species are ONLY found in the ocean because they aren't land creatures. Any hot conditions would kill them right of. It is peccable that humans know that these creatures cannot land on anything other than water. Without water, these creatures would perish, therefore it is evident that the effects of climate change on these previous ecosystem's points to the fact that without sustained water, mammals of this kind will become extinct faster than any other species.

One would think that mammals are protected because global warming doesn't hit waters as bad as land, partly true but waters can become heated causing prime conditions for these whales to flock to other areas of the world that aren't as warm. It has to be stated that once the dolphins cannot handle any heat, then the other species will become extinct unless they find a pool of cool water somewhere that hasn't been hit by rising temperatures, the problem is by 2070, the world will be very hot everywhere.

Such a massive increase in temperature will no doubt shrink the water levels in the ocean and thus these creatures will decrease in numbers at a rapid rate. To think that these creatures won't be able to survive such conditions raises the possibility of other species that are water made become extinct with the dolphins. Such other species are crucial to having the water environment protected from rising temperatures, the only issue is to note and examine how hot is enough for these water creatures? They cannot survive in desert-like conditions because it is too hot, the lack of water means in these locations, they are not any lakes or rivers because it is way too hot and never rains.

The 9th species at risk of extinction is eastern Himalayan mountains because they are natural protected areas that won't be able to withstand changes in the climate. These mountains are a good source of viewing because they have birds and other species that carry food to other species. If this species were likely to become extinct then the whole other air species would suffer a mass extinction due to climate change. The scary reality is that this sacred place in the world has been around for a long time and if global warming destroys this habitat, then it would cease to exist.

The 10th species at risk of extinction is Giant Panda which originate in climates where it is usually rainy. Such creatures cannot take the heat as their fur only withstands cool conditions that aren't prime to become as hot. The reality being if this species is threatened by climate change, then all pandas will not be able to survive the rising temperatures. Thus, it is evident that because of the rising global warming, these species are dying other slowly. The worry is by 2070, there will not be any pandas across the globe, they will already be gone. To summarize how scary of a picture this points to the reality that something must be done to save these creatures, there are campaigns to save the panda. Such campaigns aim to promote a safer and more protected environment for such creatures before climate change wipes all of them out.

The 11th species at risk is Monarch butterfly meaning these creatures that thrive in flowery conditions won't be able to adapt to the rising conditions met with climate change. Such species are crucial to the habitat of other species of the insect nature. Bees, wasps and other species need these butterflies to protect them from the larger species that would threaten them. With climate change becoming more real and wicked, these small species would become extinct due to rising gases and other factors such as lack of flowers to pollinate due to rapid rise in temperature. There needs to be temperature climate to promote these creatures because if it gets too hot quickly, these creatures will not be able to survive.

The 12th species at risk if the polar bear thus these creatures only thrive around the north pole. Such a climate is only seen up north because it is only ice and snow and being nothing else. These creatures cannot survive in anything but ice and snow because that is how their body is equipped to handle. If they were to migrate south, they would perish because of the lack of ice and snow. Polar bears aren't common in Canada because it is too hot, the farthest north one can go is to find polar bears.

It is natural to find such creatures safe from the effects of climate change because it doesn't even warm-up in these climates, therefore nothing is able to grow because it is so cold. However, once the ice starts to melt due to rapid warming which is already starting to occur in parts of the north like the arctic. Sea ice is melting due to warmer temperatures, so it is only a matter of time until all the ice and snow is gone. Polar bears therefore would not be able to make it and would perish and become extinct.

The 13th and final species at risk of climate change are sea turtles which go in line with other water creatures. Thus, these creatures need mostly swamp to be able to live. Swamp is created when rain becomes heavy and causes such an environment. However, with the planet warming at an alarming rate, there isn't as much rain and usual and thus the swampy conditions aren't met, therefore the species of turtles cannot thrive in such conditions if swamp isn't met with water. Thus, the rate of mass extinction among these species will be great if the waters don't become swamp due to heavy rain which will happen with rapid global warming.

The final thought is that all these species at risk of extinction due to climate change point a picture that isn't rosy. The planet is already starting to see such species lower in numbers due to it becoming warmer with each passing decade. The worry going forward is how the WWF will create campaigns to try and save the earths most endangered species because if the science is right about the rate of climate change by late 21st century, these species will be no more. Just imagine a planet without any birds, mammals and animals, it will be like nothing but humans before all of humanity is last to go. Without the cooldown, the world will shrivel all the species that it needs to thrive. Time to adapt to the reality of the mass extinction which has already begun.

CHAPTER 12

The reality is that all the talk over the last 11 chapters has been on the effects of climate change and what the world is doing in terms of combating the problem. To say that this world isn't doing anything to combat climate change is adequate because quite frankly this globe doesn't care about the future. If this is true, then our planet and the people in it don't think about the solutions to the problem because their tactics to reduce emissions and greenhouse gases fail in comparison to the reality of an issue that isn't going away. Humans need to realize that their ways of combating climate change aren't working and thus more needs to be done, there are solutions to the issue but already thinking about solving such problems don't seem relevant to your average joe.

To state that humanity is not solving climate change is worrying because if nothing is done, then our planet will continue to suffer the way it has and it will not be able to sustain any kind of effort from people to resolve what is already occurring. Humans don't need to think about the solutions that will be discussed here, but to promote them because if it doesn't work, then we cannot fix the problem, therefore there is no point of any effort due to the reality that this precious world will become extinct and too hot. Humans need to then be able to adapt to the new norm which is the next chapter but for now is trying to find solutions before it gets to a stage of no return.

The 1st solution is Eliminating or stopping fossil fuel burning meaning all the gases C02, methane, natural gas and even other gases used for work. The problem here is that humans need the above gases to survive because this world relies on such gases to function. Therefore, it is evident that people aren't going to give up these gases or using them because it is their daily lives and the activities accumulated during these hours. It will be very hard to convince people to stop using natural gas because this is what heats their homes in the winter season. People need to stay warm in cooler months and therefore need this type of gas. As well as those who work in industrial areas need certain gases to keep making products that will benefit the community. If production is stopped, then those products will not be made and thus effecting the economy at large.

Such issues point to the reality that humans need fossil fuels to survive but there is hope that if humans can stop using these fuels in selfish ways, the climate will adapt and stop warming. The problem is because our side of the globe is richer than the rest of the world, our continent of North America is the richest in the world, and therefore uses the most gases. Such that if we can somehow reduce our need to use these gases, it would benefit both the society that we live in and the climate in general. However, people aren't going to stop using these gases right away until an alternative is introduced that will replace these fossil fuels. For example, energy efficient items are a source to look at that don't use gases or fossil fuels. There are things that can be done, but people need to change their tune and think of alternatives to natural gas, something like heat built it to the unit, like a baseboard that heats up the whole house or room.

Part of the solution could be wind driver systems that could power homes instead of electricity. It is a safer and energy efficient way to reduce hydro bills and the effects of power outages. When the power goes out, people use generators and fuels just to make it, however if they change to wind power, then there won't be a need for electricity and the gases of generators during power failures. Each time these gases are burned, they release chemicals that pollute the air, doing what is right to combat this issue takes time and courage in the face of the reality that people must become aware of what gases they are using to heat their homes. The final thought is that if we are to combat the problem of fossil fuels, we must realize that our ways need to change in what we do. If we can change our ways of thinking, then it is possible to reverse some effects that the fossil fuels have on the planet. It will take time because people have done the same things for centuries.

The 2nd solution is infrastructure upgrade meaning building more energy efficient homes and buildings. Such that if one were to look at the emissions that cement causes to the atmosphere once introduced will no doubt lead to a crisis. The reality of what it would take to build homes that don't use cement or other materials that are toxic to the air. Think about the reduction of costs to buy or rent the units in the building if they were energy efficient. It only takes some intelligent thinking to create such buildings that don't need cement or concrete but are energy efficient. If we are to tackle climate change, first are foremost is the focus on less chemical created houses, but more energy-based products. Every time a construction worker drills a hole or pounds a nail into a wall, they release dust that will trigger effects that aren't good for the air and health of people who have allergies.

We need alternative fuels to heat the homes because the current ones only add to the greenhouse gases. If we continue to use such fuels to heat the homes we build, then those greenhouse gases will continue to pollute the air leading to the sun causing more warming and extreme weather events that will get worse. A contractor must think about this before building a house, but no one knows how to even comprehend the effects of such a mess until the globe experiences the poor choices of humanity. Such homes need to be constructed with the mind of energy saving, thus reducing greenhouse gases being 1st priority. The likelihood of this changing is slim because most people that build houses don't use this knowledge or are unaware of the real danger or putting greenhouse gases into the air. It seems relevant then to include the reality of the effects of such ignorance because the consequences are severe and long-lasting.

In order to build better homes that use less chemicals, but energy is to think of blueprints before the design goes through for the creation of the new house. If the design goes through and it doesn't include energy efficiency, then the failure is one the person who wrote up the plan because they aren't thinking about saving the planet, they are thinking about building a house and that is it. Such lack of thought of the effects of climate change promote the reality that it will cost more money to make it energy efficient, and the developer doesn't have the cash to spend. If this is true, then it is safe to bet that those involved in the building process don't realize that there is a reality of climate change that is causing wild weather across the globe. Such a final thought would be to familiarize these folks with global warming and the effects their current behaviors are having on the planet at large, only then will they change their ways, moving on.

The 3rd solution is move closer to work; thus, you don't have to drive a lot of miles. When one drives a distance, the gases from the tunnel where it shoots our pollutes the air causing greenhouse gases to become trapped. They say that gasoline alone produces a huge amount of CO2 per vehicle. Imagine all day, cars and huge vehicles cruise down the highways creating all this CO2 and thus is released into the air across the globe, can you think of the effects of the gases? It is obvious the effects go directly to the suns core, and it is trapped causing the planet to heat up. It is serious to think that humans need to drive so much because if it is for work, then it is obvious that most people would rather commute to a larger city for work, then to move to that location. It is about saving money on housing prices because to give up living in an area that has beauty and nature seems like people don't know what they are doing.

Why wouldn't one move closer to work? If you work in Victoria and live in Duncan, why not look for a place in downtown Victoria so you don't have to drive 1 hour each day which adds up on gas and all that CO2 your vehicle is using. One cannot think about the effects of such behavior until we engage in it. If the cost of living being the factor that prevents one from moving to the same city they work in, then it is a cause for worry that people would rather save money on rent then to save the environment. The logic here is that why drive all that way just for work? Do you think that is wise? If you can find a decent place in another city that you work in, then invest in doing so, save your money. The problem is people aren't that bright in terms of saving of money, they just spend it going into debt. The average person incurs more debt in Canada than any other place globally. This is a cause for concern because what are people spending their money on? If it isn't a house, then why but that new fancy toy? You don't need it, just stop with oh I need to save money, so I don't bother moving to the same city I work in, go figure right?

There are alternative ways of transportation than driving. One can walk, take the bus, train, carpool and Sky train. The reality is if people were to switch from driving everywhere and used public transportation, then all that CO2 wouldn't be introduced into the air. Just think of the money one would save on gas and other car expenses. If one walked to work, then there is no cost for gas, no cost for expenses, and a safer mode to work, no accidents. Walking is better for one's health, it promotes a stable cause of reducing weight and you feel better walking. Yeah, it is a slower way to get somewhere, but you enjoy the journey of where you are going rather than going there fast.

Another thing is cutting back on air travel, so instead of flying, take the ferry if you desire to go long distance or eliminate long-distance travel. You save money on trips you don't need to take, if you are wise enough to understand it is better saving the planet, than indulging in a vacation that will only last 2 weeks. If it is an emergency and you must see someone, then fine or for that Christmas vacation, ok, but constant long-distance travel gets your wallet empty flying all that way. If you can, just stay home or find alternative ways to connect with others on the other side of the world, there is Facebook and social media.

If you do travel by airplane, short and medium trips for a vacation for X-mas and other holidays is fine because greenhouse gases like CO2 are not as bad as those large trips that are not necessary. It is choices like this that will promote better reality for the planet and your wallet. If you don't want to spend more than 1-2 weeks somewhere, then don't plan on to. To summarize that if everyone did their part in terms of reducing their times driving or flying, then the planet would thank us and thus greenhouse gases would be reduced into the atmosphere promoting a better future for our generations.

The 4th solution is to simply consume less of what you are currently using. This means to buy less stuff which equates to less electronics, less cars, less games, less toys, less of anything that is of luxury. Such choices are hard because our society is hooked on buying stuff to fill the void inside of them that is polluted with the reality oh this guy has the newest PS5, so I want it as well. I even have fallen trap to this reality because every store has ads that promote a craving for these items. No wonder why the stores are filled during the holidays, people need to have the newest gadgets, toys, games and other items to fill their houses.

Even groceries can add to the greenhouse effect because the bags you put your food in, causes the gases to be released into the atmosphere. Thus, having bags that don't use gases and thus are eco-friendlier for the planet is a start of a choice that will save the climate from a global catastrophe. Such choices need to be implanted because people need to understand that it is okay to reuse your bags, not create more plastic that will indeed pollute the air. So instead of plastic, use green bags, these aren't plastic, they are tougher to hold more items plus they don't create the same effects plastic bags do.

Ditch the car or vehicle is another choice that will work if people don't feel the need to have all their money earned spent on bills like insurance, gas, and fixes their car may need. It seems only certain that if people don't drive as often, then our planet would be better off without the increased flow of traffic on the roads which in turn creates more CO_2 because every vehicle uses the same gases. Solution adapt to electric vehicles that don't use gas or oil, these vehicles are already starting to hit the market, so if those items can replace the current ones, no CO_2 would be introduced into the air saving the planet.

The 5th solution is be efficient meaning you are doing the right things to save the planet does not make it worse. We waste a lot of stuff in the developing world, people throw everything in the oceans, landfills and other areas that don't need that stuff. If we could stop this, the planet could be saved, it takes the reality of caring for the planet to stop wasting the resources we have. I see garbage everyday on the streets, in the oceans, in places that shouldn't be, I see things like cardboard wasted because it is no good, Instead of recycling the things we have, we throw them in the trash when something breaks or our dirty dishes and papers as well as boxes of food that is empty.

Such effects of throwing everything away instead of recycling it promotes the greenhouse gases to be introduced into the air which causes those items to be trapped and therefore our climate suffers. People need to realize the reuse and recycle are the solutions here, if something isn't as bad, reuse it the second, third or even forth time because it is still good. You don't need to throw it out if it still has value and works. So, instead of throwing it in the trash, use it again, you save money and the planet. A second way is recycling the items if you aren't going to use them again because that is the way the materials go to a place that doesn't pollute the air. Thinking of how to recycle our items is better than throwing or discarding our items in landfills, oceans or other sources that aren't good for the planet.

If everyone were to recycle what they have, then our planet would become free of greenhouse gases thus not being emitted into the air. This is the notion that our society must change their ways of doing things before it comes to the point that our planet cannot be reversed in terms of climate change. Think about how cleaner our land areas would be if everyone reused and recycled their products once done with them, it would go a long way to reverse global warming. Thus, if people were to utilize this reality, then our planet would thank us for preserving it to the fullest, however it starts with us. We must want to make changes in how we do things, it takes only one person to start a chain of events that will lead to others following suite.

Another thing is to turn off the lights when you aren't in a room because it saves hydro bills and energy. If we all could do this, the costs of such services would go down and lead to lower greenhouse gases being emitted into the air. Such an effect would provide a stable reality that all people would benefit from lower hydro bills and less need to heat our homes. My dad always said to me when I was a teenager to turn off the lights when I am not in a room. This reignites in my brain that every time I leave my room, I turn off the lights, in fact even in the winter when it gets dark earlier, I don't have any lights on because I know hydro is more expense at that time of the year. I desire to save money on my bills because I am cautious of how much I have on; thus, I realize that saving this planet is important to me.

The 6th solution is Eat smart, go vegan. Now this may sound ridiculous that how could what we eat contribute to greenhouse effect? It seems silly to escape the reality of climate change for people who feel the need to gloss over this topic, but there is something here. When you eat the right way, your body not only feels better, it functions better. Did you know that every time one kills animals for food, it promotes greenhouse gases? It is true because those slaughtered animals cannot defend themselves from selfish humans whose only purpose is to have meat for their winter meals. It is sad that this topic must be confined to this book because I hate talking about stuff like this, but it must be discussed. How could humans need their meat so bad; they would do anything for it, it seems silly to conclude that humanity is going down the drain.

If one were to go vegan meaning less meat more vegetable, everyone would be healthier because they wouldn't be consuming all these products that promote greenhouse gases and climate change. It would make us more reliant on those healthy alternatives to meat that would promote a healthier lifestyle that people would take notice. So, choose to go vegan, stop slaughtering animals for your meat and it will save the planet and those previous creatures that are having their lives terminated by humanity that only desires to get their ways.

The 7th solution is stop cutting down trees deforesting our planet. Trees provide shade from the sun and habitat for birds and other creatures that deserve better. These creatures don't deserve their nest to be destroyed by humans, they deserve for it to be preserved. The reality is that every tree cut down promotes greenhouse gases like crazy. If the tree isn't dying, then don't cut it down, if it is still good, then keep it up. You will save the planet in doing so, there is not needed to destroy nature for your job to reduce the shade the sun rays through. If the shade is reduced, then people wouldn't be able to cool themselves down during the summer and wind wouldn't be natural effect. Such effects are noted that people who deforest don't give anything about the planet, they are only doing a job that is putting our planet in jeopardy.

Forests have habitat for many species that will become extinct if deforestation continues, thus being the problem going forward that people don't seem to think about, all they care about is using those trees to make more products that are useless for the salvage of our planet. People need to realize every time someone goes hiking or camping in the woods, they are away from the city life and free from noise. If trees keep getting cut down but selfish people, then there isn't any room for us to camp, for moose, deer and other species that live in the wild to thrive. Therefore, every species will be killed as a result of the deforestation. Do you realize how much CO_2 is released into the air from deforestation? It is a lot of tons that isn't needed because it doesn't boat well for the planet nor does it for the species already at risk with climate change.

Whenever I see people deforest an area, I get upset become that is habitat of creatures and greenhouse gases that aren't needed into the air. Such activities make me wonder what this world is coming to. Are people really that stupid to engage in such practices knowing the long-lasting effects of such activities? The reality of not caring about the effects of such practices makes one wonder, why bother plant all those trees knowing they will all be chopped to the ground.

The 8th solution is unplugging your devices and save electricity. Every time one has their electronics on, it creates greenhouse gases that are introduced into the air causing the planet to warm meaning the weather becomes more extreme and erratic. People need to understand put a limit on how much TV you watch, how many hours a day one plays their gaming systems, how much time listened to the radio and other things. If we could do this, we would save money on internet, phone and other bills that don't need to be as high. It only makes sense to ditch using electronics when you don't need to use them. If for work or school fine, but if on the internet on social media all day, it isn't a smart choice because the waste of time and money, plus you are contributing to global warming.

If one were to unplug their TV, then there wouldn't be a need to view the box and therefore one would save money on cable which is going up as well as if one didn't use the internet or unplugged that, less time on social media. Therefore, the time is spent more with friend's actual face-to-face activity plus doing other things like getting out more. Walking, hiking, camping trips are better fits than staying inside playing video games all day. It seems evident that if people don't change this way of living life, then our planet will suffer and get warmer causing massive power outages from overheated electronic activity. The more power, the more likely of a power failure due to everyone using their gadgets at the same time which overloads the circuit.

I know it will be hard considering this is the common way of interaction is through social media and is becoming more common with each year. It is evident that our way of interaction with others has changed to the point that we aren't seeing others anymore; we are texting people instead of the old-fashioned way. Texting uses data and resources to code a message to someone that we know but, does it work? It works only for those that discover that it isn't the mode that is disturbing, it is the way we do it that is. If someone texts all day without seeing the person in real life, then how does that person know there is a connection.

The 9th solution is to have only one kid instead of many. I personally laugh at this one because I don't think I will have kids or get married. However, with one kid promotes more costs that need to be incurred to take care of that kid. The more costs mean more stuff bought for the child which in turns promotes the planet in a negative way. If you bought your kid everything they want, then you are contributing to the global crisis, and your child once they grow up will do the same thing to their kids. It only seems evident the more kids one has, the more stuff and money towards things that lead to increased global temperatures. No one realizes this because they don't think about the science behind it, it sounds crazy to assume that people who have more than one kid realize the task of satisfying their child's needs.

If you bought your kid everything they want, then you are creating the issue. Why make something worse that is already to a point of no return. Solution don't have lots of kids, it will make it easier for you as parents as well as the planet which is on edge every time these gases from your kids are introduced into the air. The reader may laugh after reading this because it is silly, how could having less kids lead to a better future for this planet. But, it is the little things that make up the puzzle, thus if you don't adjust your patterns of behavior, it seems evident that one doesn't know or realize the mess the planet is going to be in when the robots take over.

The 10th and final way to solve this crisis is promote alternative gases and future fuels that don't lead to increased CO2 being introduced into the air. Such gases are already starting to make their rounds due to the reality that climate change is real and getting worse. It seems evident that CO2 is the killer and this type of gas is the most common cause of the greenhouse effect. Therefore, humanity must realize in order to stop the effects of climate change, it seems logical to replace CO2 with something else, but what else could eliminate this gas? Hydrogen electrolyzed of water is a solution that has being studied and does have benefits.

Another thing is biofuels, and this has been started already but there are negative effects. With the introduction of such fuels, food prices will skyrocket meaning your average person will have to limit what they buy; therefore, food banks would be a source for even a middle-income earner. With the rising costs of food, people may switch to organic and fermented products that don't have as much value but in order to make their bills on time, drastic measures are needed. Such effects are the reality of the notion that people will not be able to afford anything but Kraft dinner which isn't very good for you at all.

There is an upside, more hybrid electric vehicles that don't use gas will become the focus that will lead to greenhouse gases stopped from being increased into the planet. However, there are costs to operate these vehicles replacing the current ones, it will be costly for the economy of sales for automotive because the vehicles built mostly are that of oil and gas. Such a change would spark a cleaner planet and thus these vehicles would be faster than the current ones because they don't need gas to run, they are electric which is cool.

The final thought is after considering the solutions to climate change seems evident to start creating the notions to have climate strikes to increase awareness of the effects that greenhouse gases have on the planet. If we don't find solutions to our current way of living, greenhouse gases will only get worse until they become a hot topic for debate that won't be just talk, our planet will be hotter than Mars. People need to realize that our goals in life of what we desire stems from our inability to accept the reality that our weather is more extreme than even before and the next focus coming up in next chapter is adaption to global warming and the new norm of heatwaves and droughts.

Such topics as an important note don't need to be reminded to those that choose to continue with their current ways of living, it seems evident that this world doesn't need a miracle from god, it needs people that will hold others accountable for their choices that are leading to this world becoming a place that is to hot to live and extreme weather from coast to coast of the globe. Therefore, more research is needed to convince others that global warming is real, but it can be reversed if people get off their horns and start creating a catalyst for change. If one person made changes, 2 people and 4 and 8, the list goes on. Who desires to see a world that is back to the way it was after the last ice age ended; I know I do? It takes good choices to promote the reality that will lead others to follow suite, thus we need a revolution of people that are willing to stand up and say that is enough. What you are doing is harmful, stop it only then will things change, but for now to hope climate change doesn't get to what they experts say.

CHAPTER 13

The next focus now is on how do we adapt to climate change and the rising temperatures? There isn't a clear answer because on how does the average person change to view what damage they have caused to a planet that didn't deserve such disrespect. However, it is humans that are cruel and nasty, thus being the most influential reality of our day and age, to adapt to a society and environment that is hotter and will continue to soar in degrees.

The reality is there are 6 things one needs to realize in order to adapt to the reality of man-made global warming. It is evident then that people aren't ready to adapt to what damage has already been caused due to greenhouse gas emissions into the air. People need to think about how much damage has been caused by climate change and realize that the planet will never go back to the way it was. The reality then is how best to adapt to a world that is both warmer and more dangerous in terms of stormy patterns.

It is evident then that before we discuss the reality of what the new normal will be, it is to state clearly that the current pattern of global warming is by far the worst situation in human history. Never has it been so warm and erratic weather patterns and thus it doesn't point to the end of the world, it points to the reality of a planet that is angry and will unleash its fury on the citizens because there is nothing that cannot stop what is coming for the world. Mother nature will not stop warming this planet until earth is too hot causing those that are still alive to move to another cooler planet.

The 1st reality to adapt to is more intense heatwaves thus being the new norm for even places like the BC coast. Such, that in the fall it could hit 20.C in

November which has never happened before. There has never been a year the temperature has hit 20+ in the Cowichan Valley, check the records and there isn't a year yet. However, heatwaves can occur at any time of the year, and with climate change becoming severe, it could be July in November a month that it struggles to reach the 10.C mark. Suh a abnormal trend would have impacts that have never been seen, BC will be summer in a time where the days are shorter, and the rapid daily warning will mean those ski resorts won't be able to open on time.

It is normal to have spikes in temperature between November- March due to pineapple express systems causing rain and high winds, but a heatwave hitting 20+ would be something that could happen every year. It is scary that this could happen in BC at this time of the year, usually winter starts in November when the temperature goes below 10.C and it gets dark around 4:30. However, thinking about the effects of the heatwaves in the winter is something that isn't talked about because they occur between April- October which is the spring-fall season. In fact, it doesn't start hitting 20.C until later in the spring, but with global warming, it could be year-round. This wouldn't be normal for anywhere in Canada to hit 20.C in winter because usually it is known to hit the double digits, but not the 20s.

Heatwaves in the summer will be so bad, it will be just as hot as Arizona. You won't be able to go outside due to it being so hot, thus what activities would one be able to do with it being so scorching? Exercise indoors would be the new norm in the summer season and even the lakes would be too hot due to heatwaves for swimming and boating. This scary picture is the reality of something we must adapt to as the new norm. With the recent decade in BC having nasty summer heatwaves, it is only a matter of time till this world planet is scorching in the summer. Arizona could be all over most of the world in places like the Middle East which would be scary and worth debate.

Heatwaves cause so many health issues as discussed earlier but could become deadly due to climate change with it reaching temperatures in the summer that it never reaches. BC never has been above 50.C during the summer and one can imagine reaching this in July, now that would be freaky. Think about even 60.C in summer in places like the Middle East as daytime highs, that would be no one working or doing anything outside, time to build homes that are cold enough built in air conditioning because that is how bad it could get if the models get warmer.

Such heatwaves could cost the economy millions of dollars in lost productivity and wages. It would be a ripple effect on whatever direction the globe takes in terms of how hot it is, and thus this increased heat will no doubt make us extinct. Species will not be able to survive, it will be a picture of horror because of the effects of such warming on a planet that is already warm enough just imagine how warm 5.C could be? It will be dramatic increase in sickness and suffering because humans aren't able to adapt to such warming due to our internal temperature being only able to withstand so much.

The 2nd new norm is more rain in the fall-winter season being so severe, every year it floods and causes landslides. We already have this happening in parts of the globe due to increased water temperatures, time to adapt to what could be drastic in terms of how much rain will be added. The storms in BC are bad in the rainy season and with global warming increasing, the risk of having more severe rainstorms that are long-lasting seems evident. Can you imagine it raining on BC coast for 30 days straight non-stop, this would cause major flooding and records to pile up with all that rainstorms? Those systems usually have breaks, but with the new norm of climate change, these storms will not only be back-to-back, they will be larger. Larger meaning the size of 3* what they are now, this being rain solid throughout the day and night for a week until it stops.

When it rains, people don't go outside because it is too wet, so if it becomes very bad, we might have to invent something stronger than regular umbrellas that would be guarding the rain. Rain is common during the colder season due to the increase in activity in the Pacific, but if climate change worsens, these storms will become stronger due to warmer waters which is interesting. However, even with all these storms means that we will have abundant water for the winter season thus leading the boil water advisories each year. These advisories will be a nuisance to all those people that rely on water for their businesses and activities. Such a reality is starting to take shape, those fall storms are nastier and bringing more rain, think 50 years in the future how bad or the new norm those people will have to face, it will be awful.

The 3rd new norm is nasty droughts in the summer caused by lack of rain. Such events are already starting to happen today, but with the new norm of climate change, it could be drought 8 months of the year. This will cause many farmers to give up planting anything knowing it won't make it through and thus to chuck everything that was planted earlier in the season. This is how serious it could be for other areas of the world that cannot plant such produce due to it being a desert-like atmosphere. If global warming becomes as they predicted, it will cause the growing seasons to become so long, one would be able to start planting produce in the winter. Drought is a major topic that has been around in BC and is worsening each year. 2019 has had the worst drought in BC due to climate change and this will be the new norm every year.

Think of how bad our droughts are now and think in 50 years how bad they will be, it will be no water to drink during the summer. How would one survive without water? We would have to invent a system like going to the mountains to get water due to lack of it. Water restrictions wouldn't just be for summer, they would linger all the way up to December due to climate change being the scary reality of a world that will be drying out. If the increase in droughts is scary, think about what it would take for us to adapt to the new normal of this occurring? We would have to prepare for a summer of no water, this sounds absurd, but is the reality. BC in 2019 had a record year for drought and this signal of drier than normal pattern isn't going away due to a high-pressure system that because of global warming is becoming more stagnant. The concern is that other places across the world that aren't accustom to drought will experience them on a regular basis been more severe. Much work must be done to combat this reality because other planet is in dire need of water. The drier summers is linked to global warming and this has happened before with the last warm period, but the current one is much worse.

The 4th new norm is nasty windstorms that will become more extreme and frequent. Windstorms in BC have been very bad over the last 5 years especially one in late 2018 that caused a lot of damage. The reality is that the windstorms will become so severe, that it will be hurricane force evens that are every fall-winter period in places like the east coast of Vancouver Island. It states that our planet and the windstorms would be a major news story because if global warming is causing these wicked yearly windstorms, what strength would they be in 2070? Wicked windstorms are the new normal and it is time to face the reality of them occurring every year. Such a scary reality would freak anyone out because no one wants to experience such events. I know I don't like windstorms, cause every time one happens, I get scared.

It is not just here in BC; it is worldwide that will experience such events because no one is immune to global warming and its wrath. Such places that aren't used to such events would be shocked to have them occur. Wind is natural in response to an ongoing system that is typical for the colder seasons, but the wind speeds will become nasty and leading to watching the trees sway all the way over. The freaky scene would cause people to want to run away because the thought of the trees falling to the ground would be high. We could have these events in hot summer months where one day it could be 30.C and heatwave and the next day 115kph winds with a high of 25.C. It seems evident then that these freak windstorms are the result of a new norm that is already taking shape, and will no doubt hamper the reality of our peaceful life.

The 5th new norm is more nasty snowstorms that bring heavy amounts of snow and blizzard-like conditions resulting in loss of work and school. In 2019, BC had the worst February on record for snowfall. It was so bad; one would walk down the sidewalk and see a foot of snow that was plowed right up to the curb of the street. Walking through fields with 1.5 feet of snow is hard enough but could one imagine 3.5 feet of snow? This is how bad it could get because those moisture events are becoming nastier causing with its intensive snowsqualls that are hitting even the BC coast. The BC coast prior to 2019 has never had snowsqualls, but with climate change becoming worse, anything is possible.

It is not just this part of the world; it is everywhere that has winter. Winter is nasty due to the Jetstream at that time of the year causing with it such conditions, but it has never been so snowy. The places that are hardest hit will become the new norm for every winter. What worries me is that 2019 will be happening in 2020 in terms of snowy conditions in BC. BC has already had a colder fall in 2019, so it is a matter of time till it snows, it could be late-November when the first event happens in 2019 after what was the worst winter on record in parts of BC. BC used to be mild in the winter without much snow, but recently for the last 3 years it has been cold and snowy. This is the worrisome trend that leaves one wondering what is next? Will it snow in the summer? If so, then global warming is causing these patterns to occur meaning something isn't right about the planet? However, people of course don't care too much, they just do whatever they can to avoid facing the new normal.

The 6th new norm is rising sea levels that will not only hit the USA but even on the west coast of BC. Rising sea levels are a new normal that is already taking shape in many parts of the world due to increased global temperatures. What will it be like in 2070? It could be so bad, those places like Tofino BC could be underwater. Such a reality points to the cause for concern among people who enjoy the visiting of such places. Such places and the beaches are a harbor for people during warm summer months that enjoy water activities including swimming. With climate change being nasty, the new norm of rising sea levels along the BC coast will no doubt cause these people who enjoy such activities to rethink what they do in the summer. They won't be able to go swimming because the beach isn't there, it is just water.

Other areas around the world like Mexico aren't being impacted quite yet, but as we know it is only a matter of time until such places are not your vacation destination due to the rising sea levels which seem to be only getting worse. Such effects are evident in people who desire to get away from cold winters in Canada, but with the new norm of rising sea levels, even ferries would not be able to adapt to that kind of thing. It is scary to talk about, but the new normal of these conditions seems evident that people need to try and save our precious planet before it becomes as bad as they predict.

So how does one adapt? This question seems evident that more research in needed to explain to people that climate change is on the news every week and this is the 1st thing people see when they turn on the TV. Such a reality points to the notion that we cannot adapt because humans aren't used to such conditions becoming frequent due to the past that wasn't as hot. Therefore, it is safe to assume that humanity isn't ready for the reality of a planet that isn't able to sustain anything other than desert-like plants. For those who think the above effects won't happen because somehow greenhouse gases will stop, think again, they will never cease. So, what does one do to prepare for these events? The question is more than just thinking about, it is about putting into perspective based on what is happening now and how bad the future will be.

The reality of adapting seems like getting that emergency kit ready because with all the wicked weather, it seems that these events will occur and thus create lots of days where one would wish it wasn't so. However, to adapt to a reality that has being going on for ages, seems evident of how the people back in 900-1300 during the last warm period adapted? They didn't have the things we have today because it didn't exist. Technology back then wasn't existent to deal with the effects of climate change, had those people would have been alive today, it wouldn't be their deal to make it through. However, to adapt to the new normal is more than just changing our ways of living, it is accepting what will happen every year. Therefore, we need to prepare for it before it happens.

How does one prepare for these events? It isn't possible to explain but every year do the same things before the summer hits for drought and have a good supply of fire fighting materials just in case, because it could be a very nasty forest fire season. Such events will happen every year due to climate change and it is best to prepare during the winter before summer hits. Therefore, before the wildfires start, one must realize that lots of stuff is needed to be able to put out fires and prevent homes from being threatened by fires.

The reality is that people are doing things that haven't been done before because knowing that come those ripe seasons where the conditions will be favored to become the new norm of insanity point to the feature of humanity preparing for anything. If we don't prepare, then all hope is lost because let's face it, even in years where it seems like 2019 which wasn't a very nasty forest fire season in BC due to a wet summer, it isn't going to spare us every year. In 2020, BC could have the nastiest driest spring-fall on record due to global warming. Who knows what to expect but due to the new norm, expect the same?

The weather should change from year to year, so why will it be the same? It is because of global warming that is creating the new normal of weather that the planet hasn't seen before. It points to a reality of people failing to understand the logic behind how they are to prepare and adapt to such changes that only will become noticeable and create the reality of a climate that is always the same each year, no change which is the new norm that is starting to happen worldwide.

The final part of this is there anything that can be done? As stated, we may have already destroyed the planet so much, it probably is too late to reverse any effects already experienced with climate change. The globe is already at the stage of weather that will cause a stagnant pattern every year. However, people need to understand it is not all gloomy, there are things that can be done to salvage the future. We can look at the solutions discussed in the last chapters and start abiding by them. The reality is that not all gloom and doom follow, it is still hopeful the planet will stabilize eventually. However, when that occurs remains to be seen, I don't think it will happen for a while because this hot pattern is locked in. If it is so locked in, it won't change, then we just must adapt to it until something breaks it like a series of eruptions or something like a change in water circulation.

The final thought is to realize that this adaption to global warming isn't something that we desire to talk about, it is something that is evident. How can we think it isn't when one sees the news headlines are extreme weather from global coast to coasts? It seems logical then to accept the responsibility that we are to blame and therefore we need to find the reversal to what is becoming something that will continue until what happened in 1300 happens again. Eventually the globe will drift into another ice age ending this pattern, but until then to adapt to the new normal already at work and try to live as comfortable as possible.

CHAPTER 14

So, what have we learned about climate change? The reality is that everything about this topic has the focus on the notion that now we know why the climate is the way it is. We realize that our choices have impacted this planet to an extent thus being the most common reason to discover how best our choices impact the planet at large. Every time we make a choice to deforest the earth or pollute it by putting our waste into landfills and oceans, our planet suffers the consequences of such behaviors. There is a reality of a list of things we are doing that is contributing to the issue and therefore needs to be addressed if we desire this planet to revert to the way it was. To say that this will never happen is adequate meaning every effort to curb climate change is met by opposition because our choices are used to be the way they are.

Such, we need to realize that global warming is real and a major threat to the future of our planet and the species most impacted by poor human choices. Each time we do things that aren't causing a catalyst for good change, we forego the responsibility to protect the planet that god so graciously created for us to enjoy. The learned reality that global warming isn't due to natural cycles of the earth, it is due to man. Man has caused all the warming in the current period and thus being a cause to ponder what and if can be done now? It seems relevant to create a list of things that we have learned because all that we know is that our behavior is the leading cause of what our earth is feeling. It is out of sync because we created it to be that way. We have not stewarded this earth the way our ancestors protected it. To realize that our result will be drastic causing this planet that is beautiful created to cease to be such that way.

The 1ˢᵗ thing we have learned is that you cannot waste all your food items and garbage. Every time we waste food or throw stuff out that doesn't need to be tossed, the climate suffers. All those gases release into the air and create a catalyst for such nasty events that is causing climate to warm and weather to become erratic. The point to get across is why would you waste everything? If you aren't going to use it or buy it, then don't. The reality is that why not recycle it? We don't recycle because we think of nothing will happen; it is just plastic. If this was the case, then there wouldn't be any need to even care, but there are organizations that encourage recycling of items that we won't use anymore.

The other issue that gets me mad is why do we waste food? How can such a rich continent waste so much food? There are kids and people starving because of lack of food. Every time we throw food away, it is bad for the food industry, it is bad for the world at large: the people in it that are living in dire poverty and the climate because it creates a breeding ground for diseases and other infections to those homeless that have no choice but to eat out of the garbage. I've seen homeless do this and it makes me cry because how can people be so selfish? If you aren't going to eat it, then DON'T BUY IT. The apology of the bold letters indicates the need to have a society that isn't wasteful of the food that companies bring in. The economy and planet suffer because all this food is wasted and the gases in the food. Did you know there is CO_2 in certain food and drinks? One wouldn't know this due to ignorance and the reality that they get food for the craving, not for the enjoyment.

Then you have people who throw chemicals into the rivers and lakes polluting it. That is why all the salmon are dying? They don't have a nice atmosphere to spawn. These creatures are what the first nations people caught and ate. The first nations are protectors of the waters on this side of the world because they were the first human species to come to Canada. Why then would you disrespect the native people? What did they do? They didn't do anything that would cause people to throw their chemicals in oceans, lakes and rivers. If you want to fish in the summer or year-round, don't throw your waste of chemicals and other dangerous liquids into sources of water. These sources of water have species that need clean water to survive. If they don't have that, they won't be able to make it. In fact, BC has had a major reduction in water species due to climate change and increased activity of people who throw their chemicals into the bodies of water.

The final thought of this 1st topic is to realize that humans are the focus on their poor choices to not recycle what they use, to throw things out that DON'T need to be chucked. Therefore, this planet reaps the consequences of such actions and thus the species impacted become lower in number. As a result, the actions of such people create a breeding ground for the planet to not become happy and reacts in a negative way. If only everyone would take it seriously the threat of what not recycling and not throwing waste into bodies of water would do for this world, then we would have a cleaner world that wouldn't be polluted with such garbage. People need to grow up and think about the choices they make because if they continue like this, this whole world will be so polluted, it will be impossible for anything to survive without suffering ill effects.

The 2nd thing learned is that deforestation is the leading cause of it getting hotter. Think about every time one cuts a tree down, think about the species in that trees that lose their habitat. Think about what shade is reduced when the sun shines. Plus think about that trees provide shade and wind that cools the planet from overheating. If you deforest a tree that isn't dying or in danger of hitting power lines, DON'T CUT IT DOWN. If it is healthy and has birds and other species in it, keep it. Why deforest an area of land with trees? Trees and shade are what makes our planet beautiful in nature. If nature isn't guarded by humans, then the reality of a hotter planet seems evident. We learn from our choices and those that involve endangering species with deforestation and reduction in trees creates a catalyst for the gases released into the air. If one would think about this issue before they deforest, then society would reap the benefits of not having our precious greenery destroyed by human related activity.

The reality of deforestation is the problem that society needs to address, to learn about the effects of such practices having on the planet and to develop an alternative way to conduct business. The trees don't need to be chopped down, they need to stay up, and more trees need to be planted to replace those deforested by human activity. If a storm brings down a tree fine, but humans deliberately causing this seems foolish because the effects are widespread on the planet. The learning of what not to do seems that people don't care about their actions of deforestation since this tree needs to come down because their boss told them to do it.

Think about how many species are at risk when you cut down trees? There are so many negative effects of such behavior, but people don't learn from their mistakes and keep repeating them. Why repeat the same thing over again? You do it because you don't know any better, since no one taught you the correct way to engage in behavior. Your parents, friends, and teachers never raised you to be like this. It was your culture or society that brainwashed you into thinking that this behavior is acceptable because it is part of your job. That job of cutting down trees is selfish because it doesn't do anyone any good. If you would think about such a choice, then you would be able to correct it before it got to the point of no return.

The final thought with what learned about deforestation is that this planet is losing shade meaning it is hotter and there is no escape in parts of the world where it is all desert. Such that we need to realize that this practice is dumb and creates a shake your head reality that has to be erased for humans to live in peace and not suffer heat related illnesses in poor parts of the world that don't have the resources to plant trees. Think about how many people need shade to conduct their daily activities, reading a book, just relaxing, and with the lack of it creates a breeding ground for sickness due to the heat. If people would stop cutting down trees, our planet wouldn't need to overheat because those trees would cool it down. Why would anyone want to cut down trees when they provide a safe environment for species that deserve a bright future. If you stop and think about this practice and keep those trees upright, this world wouldn't be in so much trouble.

The 3rd thing learned is that driving everywhere isn't the long-term idea because too much CO2 is released into the air with every vehicle. If you don't need to drive, then don't drive, walk and take the bus, carpool or train. Something other than driving prevents those gases from being released into the air. If people are to stop this behavior and change their mode of transportation, then we wouldn't have the planet so heated up. Every time you drive, every vehicle because it is gas, relies on fuel to function. However, if we created electric hybrid vehicles that would be better for the economy and health, global warming wouldn't be so bad. We have learned that the driving of these vehicles that use gas promotes a planet that will continue to promote greenhouse gases until this planet is not going back to the way it was.

The learning curve here is the examine do you need to drive. If the answer is no, I don't need to drive everyday with no purpose, then simply don't do it. Why drive 15 minutes to a place when you can walk there. There are too many cars on the road and each day people just drive aimlessly around the cities and towns and highways. All that CO2 has nowhere to go but up into the air, so if you don't need to drive, then just leave that car at home. If it is an emergency or you need to work, then fine but if you drive because you like your vehicle and the newest features, then there is a problem. The problem lies in the reality that society is bent on finding the next vehicle that will provide them with what they need to enjoy their life. Such that if all those newer vehicles are created to promote this reality, then people haven't learned anything. People haven't learned that their driving choices is emitting all these gases into the air. Why would I care? Everyone must play their part in preventing the climate crisis from getting to the point of every election topic. In fact, climate change is the number 1 election topic for Canada because it is so noticeable with all the weather we have had.

The final note here is to examine the need if one is content on driving for the sake of it, to raise the price of gas to the point that their wallet starts feeling the effects of such behavior. What will it take then? Will they go broke? These are two possibilities that will get those people out of the cars and into public transportation. It seems that our world doesn't want to learn from their mistakes and choices and reverse them, so therefore it seems logical that our world needs to put in drastic measures to ensure that people realize what driving without any purpose would do. A vehicle isn't a mode to drive around, it isn't a luxury we enjoy, it is something that we need to want to do correctly without thinking about the goodness of being inside a vehicle. I don't have a vehicle and never will because driving is no something I would ever do. I like to stay in shape and protect the environment from increased gas emissions from vehicles. I think this world would be better off without gas powered vehicles, time to go electric hybrid.

The 4th thing learned is how better to ensure that species can adapt to the increased greenhouse gas emissions which are increasing the temperature causing many to become either extinct or reduce in number. Salmon are lowering in number because of the effects of the rivers, lakes and oceans being polluted, air creatures are threatened by deforestation, tough creatures are being threatened by heatwaves and rising temperatures, polar bears and other snow species are being threatened by reduction in sea ice. Such a reality is the learned focus that our understand of what is happening isn't registering in our brains.

We see these species and don't care too much because they aren't human thus aren't as strong. However, these creatures have feelings and suffer the same ailments that we do and anything that threatens us, will no doubt threaten them even more because their bodies aren't able to readily adapt to such changes. How then can we promote a stable environment for them that isn't too hot when our world keeps overheating. These creatures are part of gods creation and yet with our ways of living, these mammals will not be able to survive another century. The reality then is that I care about these creatures because they provide food for us. Think about where one gets their meat from, chickens, pigs, deer and the list goes on. If these mammals reduce in number, we wouldn't get our meat, therefore our minerals would become lower.

The final thought here is that all creatures deserve a planet that harbors their growth and well-being, they don't deserve to have their habitat threatened or in any way destroyed by humans who don't care about anything but making money. These creatures don't make any income because they aren't as advanced as the homo sapiens. If humans are the most predominant species outweighing all the others, then it seems evident to promote an understand that our ways of doing things is directly impacting those species. If we would learn what it would take to achieve such results, our species wouldn't need to protect their habitat from humans and those human beings would become friends with the other species. That is what god originally intended not just for man to get along with man, but for man to get along with animal.

The 5th thing learned is How climate change impacts human beings. The reality is that even though the homo sapiens are the most advanced in terms of IQ and ability, it seems evident that humans can survive anything which is wrong thinking. Humans are just as able to experience the effects of rising temperature and do so much greater than other species because of the lack of fur. Fur on an animal protects them from overheating, this fur stops the heat from getting inside causing them to feel uncomfortable. Therefore, if our bodies aren't adaptable to rising temperatures as the normal temperature is 37.C or 98.6 F. This is higher in humans then in animals but still have greater negative effects being the focal point that humans aren't able to adapt to anything over 37.C. Anything over this amount would start causing distress among the homo sapiens being the reality that we aren't as strong as once assumed.

However, human beings have been known to find ways to survive in the past warm periods, so maybe they can do the same in the future to curb the effects of rising temperatures which only seem evident. This is where humans need to learn of ways to protect themselves and if it gets to 37.C, that they find ways to stay cool which they can just as other species. However, the point of discussion is that humans need to understand what it would take for them to realize that it is too hot. Why wouldn't humans feel such need to change? It is not rocket science, it is common sense to think about the lessons that have to be learned before humans succumb to the effects of climate change. Do we want robots taking over the world? Thus, being the only species that can survive because these robots don't feel heat because they are solid and tinfoil. Thus, if robots take over the human species, then it will be a hot 22nd century that would only have robotic human species providing a stable environment where those only species in the world. Movies that point to robots taking over are becoming the new focal point and even these things are being created as we speak, so it's a matter of time.

The 6th and final lesson learned is that one cannot change just on their own, they need others that are willing to step aside and look at the effects of climate change and think how bad can it get? What should I do about this? How can we address this? A solution would be to get others involved in your actions, by climate striking. This activity raises awareness that climate change is real and getting worse. It promotes a code to follow, the more people that sign up and climate strike, the more chance that local governments, provincial and federal governments respond creating targets to be met. If we can get lots of people interested in change, then who knows where it will take us. We could lead seminars and speak on stage of the effects of global warming and what has been learned about everything that is happening and will continue to get worse. The issue is how do we address the opposition that doesn't want us to protest or become activists for change? We need to revolution of officials that will walk alongside us on the same journey to promote a better planet that will reverse global warming.

The next topic would be to do things ourselves that would promote a cleaner planet, not wasting what we have and preserving our oceans and lakes. I would say sign a petition that no animals get killed due to hunters, that we stand up against such abuse towards animals and think this is so wrong. If everyone would agree that human related hunting activities are creating the problems, then it seems evident that the next focus would be on education people of better ways to get their meat.

There are other things one can do like act against polluting the planet, such as making laws that prohibit people from throwing stuff in landfills and oceans. Therefore, there would be consequences if people broke the law, meaning jail time or a fine. Such that would enable people to not engage in such behaviors because knowing what we have learned about climate change seems plausible to assume that humans are 100% to blame. Therefore, if we can stop things like deforestation and other deliberate related activities that in tune would destroy the planet, go for it.

Another thing was to educate people on global warming since most citizens don't know what the whole thing is about. To learn why the planet is heating up like it is and to understand the causes and effects before change is made. The governments need to set goals and meet those targets. Canada is lagging in any goals and achievement of such goals because their tactics aren't strong enough to combat rising temperatures. USA is better off, but still way down there in terms of promoting a cleaner planet. Education is critical for everyone to understand what the future will be if they don't stop doing the things that the problem creates. One cannot force someone to change their ways of doing things, it takes a group of organizations to band together and say enough is enough.

The final thought would be what most learned is that we need to become more conscious of what is happening because it is real and getting worse. There isn't any plan and games anymore, this thing is as real as aliens. The reality of climate change is hot on the topics and with the weekly news with weather being the focus is a cause to think about how it came to all of this. People need to understand what is going on before they start to think about how we are going to reverse what has already happened. Or can it be reversed? The short answer is yes and no because there are points that our planet has already warmed to a state that has never happened before. It is also a hope that it can be stalled meaning it won't be as rapid as originally thought. This is the hope that we need to have going forward if any changes are going to be made because learning about the effects will drive us to desire change. The more people interested and concerned means more changes will be enacted. So, the election issue should be focused on global warming 1st thing we do something about. I am sick of global warming being 1st on the news due to the reality that it wasn't like this 100 years ago. The focus was on war, not climate change, but people have created a problem that will not stop until it is addressed. To summarize, be the catalyst for change, if you desire to change the world you will. We need to grow up and realize how bad do we want it? How bad will it get depends on us, so think about that going forward.

CONCLUSION

This book talked about global warming and everything one needs to know about a planet that hasn't ever been as hyper. Our planet has told us clearly it doesn't like what we are doing to it and everything we do causes it to become angry. Thus, humanity needs to clearly state the following as to why they continue to disobey mother nature and engage in activities that hurt her atmosphere. It seems that all people care about is the destruction of a planet that only needed love and nurture. Such wickedness points to us not being able to identify with what we need to do to realize our system of doing things must change in order to realize how bad it currently is.

The focus on the book has been to educate people and the global audience of the reality that this threat of climate change is real and not something to gloss over. It is something to consider and adapt to the reality that our world isn't going to roll over and allow us to damage it anymore. It is stating clearly that we are to blame for everything it experiences because it cannot sustain anymore abuse against it without serious consequences. These effects are becoming more common and resulting in major topics for discussion.

The planet is now hotter than it was prior to the last ice age and will continue to break records until people grow up and realize that global warming isn't a joke, it is a serious issue that will become everyday worry. The worry that people don't care seems evident that I will continue to engage in my behaviors because I don't know any better or is a pause for reflection as to why humans are so careless. They desire only what they want and not what this world wants. It seems evident that the topic of the book is to focus on what needs to be done and to do something instead of sitting around watching the world get destroyed by climate change.

One cannot just sit around and watch this world go down like this, people need to stand up and say I will do something about climate change. I don't want this for my future generations as I desire a better world that my kids will enjoy and be able to steward the way I have been taught to. Therefore, it seems real to examine not just what needs to be done, but to as stated allow people to practice a reality of global warming and pick up a book and read it like this one because it is not just about writing books, speaking on stage or changing laws, it is about REAL CHANGE THAT RADIATES AROUND THE WHOLE GLOBE.

The final thought of this book is to examine that people is not their fault that they have made such poor choices. We didn't know it would get this bad, nor did humanity forecast what their choices would do to the planet. We didn't think about it because the thought that the planet will not get as bad was the focal point. Therefore, humans aren't to blame and shouldn't be scorned at by god because they let down a planet that he created for them to enjoy. It isn't the fault of governments and big businesses for allowing these materials to pollute our seas and oceans. Humans are the smart creature that will find an end to climate change once and for all. Thus, there will be an end to this suffering but until that day comes, still I will cherish what earth I have and what god has given to those that worship him, that is the end enjoy the planet.

Printed in the United States
By Bookmasters